GCSE

A-Z

GEOGRAPHY

handbook

Steve Milner

D1392950

Hodder & Stoughton

A MEMBER OF THE HODDER HEADLINE GROUP

British Library Cataloguing in Publication Data
A catalogue entry for this title is available from the British Library

ISBN 0–340–724471

First published 1999
Impression number 10 9 8 7 6 5 4 3 2 1
Year   2003 2002 2001 2000 1999

Typeset by GreenGate Publishing Services, Tonbridge, Kent.
Printed and bound in Great Britain for Hodder and Stoughton Educational, a division of Hodder Headline plc, 338 Euston Road, London NW1 3BH, by Redwood Books, Trowbridge, Wilts

HOW TO USE THIS BOOK

Geography has its own language: various words, known as terms, belong to the subject. These terms have meaning to geographers, and to be really successful at GCSE Geography requires you to be comfortable working with this language. The Classification and Use of Terms section towards the end of the book arranges all the terms explained in the book under 15 main GCSE topic headings before illustrating this point about geographical language and GCSE Geography. I have included parts of GCSE questions which either:

- directly ask for a definition of a term; e.g. 'What is the *"dependency ratio"'*? or
- require a term to be understood before the question can be properly answered; e.g. 'Explain the significance of an increasing *dependency ratio* for an MEDC you have studied'.

Remember also that one of the features of excellent examination scripts is the introduction of suitable geographical terms, which are not used in the question, into answers. This book will help you become more familiar with geographical language so that you can use it in the examination in these three ways.

Every essential and desirable piece of geographical language you will need for GCSE Geography, whatever syllabus you are studying, is included. The terms are arranged alphabetically, and each entry starts with a simple, one-line definition. This is followed by explanation and development, often into an example of a place where the term can be accurately used to describe or explain its geography. There is extensive use of cross-referencing at the end of entries. You can extend your understanding of a term by following the cross-references printed in italics. Some of these cross-references cover different terms with the same meaning; many go much further than this and show the integrated nature of geography.

The book concludes with:

- a section on command words used in GCSE Geography examination papers. Exam success requires you to do exactly what the examiner asks you to do. If the examiner asks you to 'give reasons for' this is not the same request as asking you to 'describe'. The meanings of these command words used by the examiner when setting the questions are provided.
- a section on researching and writing up a GCSE fieldwork report. Using geographical language properly is as important in this part of the GCSE examination as in the written papers. Do the fieldwork report along the

lines given in this section, sprinkling it with well-used geographical language, and you could have up to 25% of the total GCSE marks 'in the bag' before you sit either of the written papers.

The best of luck with learning these terms!

Steve Milner

ACKNOWLEDGEMENTS

To my dear wife, Phillipa of 25 years.

abrasion: the wearing away of rocks and the ground by rock particles carried by rivers, waves, ice or the wind. It is a type of *erosion* occurring when particles carried by:
- running water scratch, scrape or scour a river channel's bed or banks
- glaciers and ice sheets act as abrasive material by rubbing away some of the ground over which they pass
- waves are hurled against cliffs and help to wear them back
- strong winds wear away rock surfaces by sandblasting.

The importance of abrasion at a particular place depends upon:
- the toughness and resistance of the rocks and ground
- the number and speed of the particles being carried.

(See also *corrasion*.)

---

absolute poverty is the most extreme state of poverty in which people lack the essential requirements for a safe and healthy life. They do not have enough:
- food
- water
- shelter
- clothing.

Those who are badly nourished in areas of famine such as in parts of the Sahel, and homeless people on the streets of British cities, experience absolute poverty.

---

accessibility: a measure of how easy it is to reach a location from elsewhere. A location that is accessible for most customers is generally chosen for activities such as superstores and medical centres. This keeps travel times and distances to a minimum. Many shops and offices choose either:
- town/city centre locations (see central business district – CBD) which are very accessible for, for instance, those using public transport, or
- motorway/ring road intersections which are very accessible for drivers.

---

acid lava is molten rock from deep within the Earth. It is thick and sticky (viscous), due to the lava being rich in silica. Acid lava flows slowly and quickly solidifies. Volcanoes formed from acid lava are dome-shaped with steep, sloping sides.

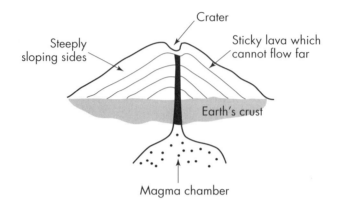

acid rain is polluted rain. Rain is naturally slightly acidic but pollution has made it more so. Acid rain is thought to harm the environment. It can cause trees to die and damage stone buildings, particularly those made of limestone, by causing them to weather more quickly. Much of this atmospheric pollution is due to sulphur dioxide and nitrogen oxide produced by:
- burning coal and oil in power stations
- smoke emissions from industry
- vehicle exhaust fumes.

There is growing pressure to reduce the output of these gases by, for example, fitting catalytic converters to cars and opening natural gas-fired power stations. (See also *permeable*, *artesian well*, *water table* and *spring*.)

adult literacy rate is the percentage of the adult population who can read and write to an acceptable standard. It is commonly used as an indicator of a country's level of development and quality of life. The different levels of development and quality of life between Britain, Mexico and Tanzania are suggested by their adult literacy rates of:
- Britain 99%
- Mexico 85%
- Tanzania 66%.

aerial photographs are taken from above an area looking down, usually from an aeroplane or helicopter. Vertical aerial photographs are taken with the camera pointing vertically down. Oblique aerial photographs are taken with the camera pointing at an angle to the ground. Heights and shapes of features and buildings are generally clearer on oblique aerial photographs but, unlike vertical photographs, the scale is not consistent.

afforestation is the planting of trees, usually where they did not grow before. An example is the coniferous (evergreen cone-bearing) trees planted around moorland reservoirs in the Pennines. They help to reduce soil erosion and also encourage leisure visitors.

ageing population: a population in which the average age continues to rise over a period of time. In *more economically developed countries* (MEDCs) such as Britain there is a growing proportion of the population aged 65 and over; our population is therefore an ageing one.

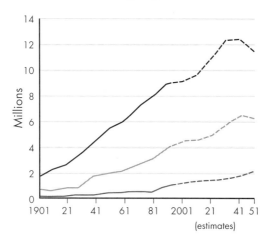

The causes are as follows.
- A low and perhaps falling birth rate – the number of babies born per thousand of the population is lower now than at almost any time in the past. Contraception is more available and attitudes to parenthood, work and spending have changed. Children are expensive to bring up and many adults want to establish a career before having children.
- Rising life expectancy – people now live longer. Diet, medicine and general living conditions have improved.

The effects
- The pattern of demand for goods and services changes.
- Providing pensions and medical care for the growing number of elderly people is becoming a real issue for many more economically developed countries; there are proportionally fewer working people to create the wealth needed to support the elderly.

(See *dependency ratio*.)

agglomeration occurs when similar firms cluster in one area which then specialises in one type of production. An example is pottery in Stoke-on-Trent. Firms can often reduce their costs by locating close to other firms or their suppliers as they may be able to link their production processes or share local services. (See *economies of scale*.)

agribusiness: a highly developed form of commercial farming. Farms are scientifically-based businesses in which:
- land is very intensively farmed
- heavy use is made of chemical fertilisers and pesticides
- mechanisation is advanced and hi-tech
- there may be production contracts with food processing companies.

Much of the non-organic British-produced food in supermarkets comes from this type of farm. (See *intensive farming*.)

agricultural revolution (new): describes the recent changes in farming in *more economically developed countries* (MEDCs), especially the change to more intensive methods of food production. Farming in MEDCs has generally become:
- more scientific and mechanised
- an employer of fewer workers
- more productive or sometimes over-productive per hectare.
- Good prices for crops are guaranteed by the government.
- So much food is produced it cannot all be sold. Mountains of food are stored in the European Union countries.
- Village communities can no longer be sustained by agriculture.
- Use of fertiliser raises crop yields but pollutes water supplies.
- Use of pesticides raises yields but damages wildlife.
- Removing hedgerows and woods to make larger fields destroys natural habitats for birds, animals and plants.

(See *agribusiness* and *intensive farming*.)

aid: the giving of resources by one country, usually a *more economically developed country* (MEDC), to another, generally a *less economically developed country* (LEDC). These resources can be, for example, gifts or loans of money, goods, food, technology or the skills and knowledge of people. The following list describes types of aid.
- Official or voluntary. Official aid is arranged by the government and paid for by taxes. Voluntary aid comes from money raised by non-government, private organisations, mainly charities such as Oxfam.

- Bilateral or multilateral. Bilateral aid goes directly to another country. 60% of British aid is bilateral. Multilateral aid goes through international organisations such as the World Bank and the United Nations. 40% of British aid is multilateral.
- Tied or untied. Tied aid has conditions linked to it, often that it is spent on goods or services from the country providing the aid. Untied aid has no strings attached to it.
- Short term or long term. Short term aid includes immediate relief for disasters and emergencies e.g. food, blankets and tents, lorries and medicines. Long term aid is assistance with development programmes e.g. road building or education and training schemes.

Some people believe that aid does harm to LEDCs e.g. it can make them dependent on aid; it can lead to tastes and habits being altered; it can create demand for imported goods. Aid money can be spent unwisely.

air mass: a stream of air with similar temperature and humidity characteristics throughout its volume. These characteristics depend on where the air has come from and what it has passed over. Air masses are linked with winds; south-westerly winds bring warm, moist tropical maritime air to Britain.

Arctic Maritime air
(very cold and dry)

Polar Maritime air
(mild and wet)

Polar Continental air
(dry, warm summer air
cold, dry winter air)

Tropical Maritime air
(warm and wet)

Tropical Continental air
(warm and dry)

alluvium: the sediment deposited by a river. Alluvium is fine material – clays, silts and sands.The flood plains and deltas of large rivers are formed of alluvium. It also occurs in formerly wet places that have dried out, beds of ancient lakes such as the Vale of Pickering in Yorkshire. Alluvium can be deposited in a cone or fan shape where a river flows onto a lowland plain from an upland valley. This is known as an alluvial fan. Alluvium is very fertile for farming. (See *delta* and *flood plain.*)

alternative energy: sources of fuel and power other than the burning of coal, oil and gas. Most of these are *renewable resources* e.g. wind power, solar power, hydro-electricity, wave and tidal power. Some countries are keen to develop such sources because they are renewable and less environmentally damaging than burning fossil fuels such as oil. (See *fossil fuel.*)

altitude: the height of a place above sea level in metres. Contours on an Ordnance Survey map show altitude. Altitude affects the weather and climate of a place. (See *contour* and *relief.*)

anemometer: an instrument for measuring wind speed. It is based on the windmill principle with the speed of rotation of the cups indicating the speed of the wind. Speeds are measured in kilometres per hour and can be stated as a *Beaufort Scale* number. (See *weather plot.*)

annotation: the labelling of a map,sketch or diagram. Clear and careful annotations are an important way in which geographers communicate information. See *acid lava*, page 2; the sketch marks the features of a volcanic dome and uses labelled arrowheads to point these out and add a note of explanation.

anticyclone: a large but temporary area of high pressure in the atmosphere, usually slow moving and lasting for a number of days. In such areas of high pressure the air is sinking so little cloud is formed. In summer these cloudless skies lead to:
- hot sunny days
- cold nights
- thunderstorms.

In winter clear night skies may lead to frost; in damp, low-lying areas fog may be formed. Anticyclones usually bring little or no rainfall. (See *radiation, thunderstorm* and *weather symbols.*)

appropriate technology describes technology given as aid to a country which is suitable for local conditions. Hi-tech equipment used in *more economically developed countries* (MEDCs) is likely to be inappropriate for a *less economically developed country* (LEDC). Inexpensive items such as a simple water carrier on wheels which saves hours a day transporting water from a well to a village may be more appropriate than an expensive pump requiring electricity. Any development arising from the use of appropriate technology is likely to be more sustainable. (See *intermediate technology*.)

aquifer: an underground layer of rock which holds large amounts of water. Rocks such as chalk and sandstone are permeable and become saturated with water. This water is used to supply people through wells and springs. It can create flooding problems for underground mining. (See *water table*.)

arable: a term which describes farming focused on the growing of crops e.g. cereals, vegetables, and so requiring the ploughing of land. An example is the cereal farming area of the Prairie Provinces of Central Canada where wheat, oats, barley and flax are grown. Most crops are spring-sown and autumn-harvested. Some are planted before winter and harvested earlier than spring-sown ones. There are:
- *cash crops*, i.e. those grown for sale
- fodder crops, i.e. those grown to feed animals.

Important to arable farming are:
- land relief – flat or gently sloping land is most suitable
- soil type – those rich in humus which retain moisture well are best
- climate – cold winters are good for breaking up the soil and warm, sunny and moderately damp summers encourage the crops to grow.

arch: a rocky coastal feature, usually found along high coastlines especially *headlands*. It forms where two *caves* on either side of a headland are eroded backwards until they eventually join. An example of a natural arch is Durdle Door along the Dorset coast. Further *erosion* leads to the collapse of the top of the arch and the formation of a stack. (See *stack* for diagram.)

areas of outstanding natural beauty are protected areas of England and Wales. They have been set aside for *conservation* because of their great natural beauty. There are 40 areas of outstanding natural beauty, among them:
- Cornwall
- the Chiltern Hills
- the Cotswold Hills
- the Wye Valley

- the Forest of Bowland
- the North and South Downs.

They are generally smaller than *National Parks* and together cover 10% of England and Wales. Conserving the natural beauty of these areas is the responsibility of the local planning authority.

arête: a knife-edged, rocky ridge found in a once glaciated upland. Arêtes form where two corries are found back-to-back on opposite sides of a mountain. An example is Striding Edge on Helvellyn mountain in the Lake District. (See *glaciation* and *corrie*.)

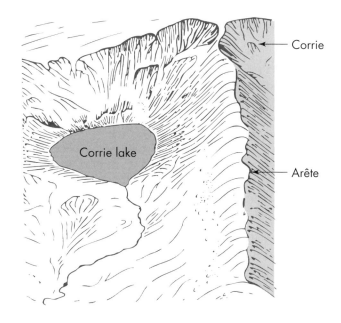

arid: this term describes a place with a very dry climate. Deserts have an arid climate; evaporation removes all the water which might have fallen as rain rendering the area too dry for plants to grow as a continuous cover. High evaporation and low rainfall are found in the hot deserts such as the Sahara. Parts of Britain can be semi-arid during dry summers. (See *desertification*, *drought* and *evapotranspiration*.)

artesian well: a well sunk into an *artesian basin*. The high water pressure in the aquifer can cause the well water to gush to the surface like a fountain. Artesian wells are found in the London Basin. (See *groundwater*.)

London basin

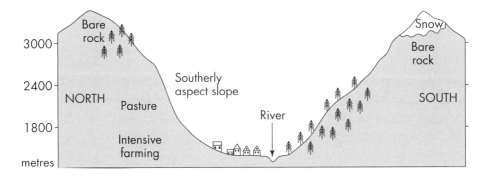

Key: ⊞⊞ Chalk   ▦ Clay   ⦾⦾ Clay wells

aspect: refers to the direction in which a feature such as a slope or building faces. Aspect changes the micro-climate of an area. For example, the temperatures on both the north-facing and south-facing walls of my house were 5°C at 8 a.m. on a winter's day. By 2 p.m. the temperature of the north-facing wall had risen to 6°C whilst that on the south-facing wall had reached 13°C. Walls and slopes with a southerly aspect are generally warmer; they are usually better for gardening and farming. The south-facing slopes of Alpine valleys are more farmed than north-facing slopes.

assisted areas: the government tries to encourage industry to set up in or move to such areas and offers financial assistance if an industry is new to the area. Higher unemployment and lower wage rates than the national average are typical of an assisted area, mainly because they:
- are suffering from the closure of old industries e.g. Merseyside or
- have little industrial tradition e.g. Cornwall or Southern Italy.

The European Regional Development Fund contributed £37 million to help with the construction of Keilder Reservoir in Northumberland. Many countries have governments who recognise and provide financial incentives for industry

in assisted areas. Government regional development agencies in Brazil offer
loans, subsidies and tax breaks to encourage firms to locate outside the South
and South East regions. (See *development area* and *enterprise zone*.)

atmosphere: the layer of gas around the Earth. The gases which make up
our air are:
- nitrogen – 79% of the atmosphere
- oxygen – 20% of the atmosphere
- others including water vapour – remaining 1%.

Most of our weather and climate occurs in the lower 7–8 miles (12 km) of the
atmosphere where water vapour exists. The atmosphere is heated from below
and *radiation* from the Sun passes through it largely unabsorbed by the air.
This radiation is absorbed by the Earth's surface which warms the atmosphere above it.

attrition: the wear and tear particles transported either by rivers and
waves or the wind. These particles collide with one another and break
down into smaller pieces. Grinding and polishing of rough particles during
transportation produces:
- fine sand which forms beaches
- smooth, rounded pebbles on river beds and along coastlines.

It is a type of *erosion*.

automation is the introduction of machinery into production. This mechanisation has taken place in many industries, especially in more economically
developed countries (MEDCs) e.g. motor vehicles, food processing, textiles,
electronics. It allows industry to:
- cut down on labour, especially where it is in short supply
- cut down on production costs in the long term after a large initial capital
  outlay
- increase output
- ensure products are of the same quality.

An example of automation is the use of robots in car factories. (See *capital-
intensive* and *mass production*.)

avalanche: a rapid fall of snow, ice and rock down a slope. Avalanches
generally occur in mountainous areas in either:
- spring when thawing lubricates snow and rock, or
- winter when fresh snow has not had chance to compact.

backwash has two meanings in geography.

- The return flow of a wave back towards the sea. Once the swash of a wave has reached its farthest point up a beach the water retreats and this retreat is called the backwash.
- The movement of resources from the less wealthy, less economically developed areas of a country, known as the periphery, to its wealthiest, most economically developed area, known as the core.

Economic backwash: resources moving from the peripheral areas to the core region will include:

- people with skills and ideas
- capital saved by people
- raw materials.

Backwash encourages the growth of the core region and widens the gap between the richer core and poorer peripheral areas. This process happens in Britain with resources moving into the core region of south-east England. It can also be seen occurring in *less economically developed countries* (LEDCs).

---

balance of trade is the difference between the value of goods exported by a country in a year and the value of goods imported by the country in that year. Goods imported and exported are called visible trade. Britain has a *visible trade*, or balance of trade, deficit, in other words, our imports cost more than our exports raise. However, trade in invisibles – services such as insurance and tourism – produces the exact opposite. We earn more than we spend on invisible trade with other countries. Invisible trade and visible trade make up a country's balance of payments.

---

bankfull: describes a river's water level at the top of its channel. When a river channel is bankfull it cannot carry any more water without *flooding* occurring. (See *discharge*.)

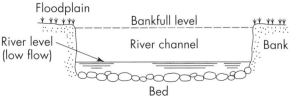

bar: a ridge of sand and shingle offshore from a coastline which:
- is formed by deposition by the sea
- can be found across the entrance to bays or the mouths of rivers
- can enclose stretches of water to form a lagoon e.g. Miami, Florida
- can move towards the coastline to form a beach as deposition of material continues.

bar chart: a diagram showing quantities as a series of vertical columns rising a horizontal axis. The various quantities are shown as columns of different height. Time e.g. years, or space e.g. countries are shown on the horizontal axis. More complicated data can be shown by bar chart when divided or multiple charts rather than the standard bar chart are drawn.

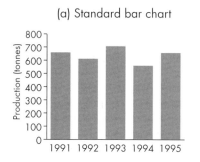
(a) Standard bar chart

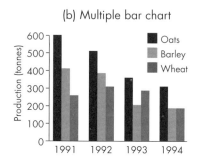
(b) Multiple bar chart

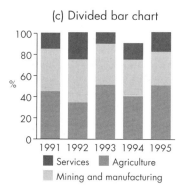
(c) Divided bar chart

barometer: an instrument for measuring atmospheric *pressure*. The pressure or weight of the atmosphere is measured in millibars (mb). The weather we experience can be related to the pressure of the atmosphere. Changes in atmospheric pressure are shown by:
- aneroid barometers with their pointers on a dial
- barographs with their graph paper tracings.
(See *anticyclone* and *depression*.)

barrage: a dam built across an estuary. This dam enables tidal power to be used as a source of electricity. The tides pass through turbines in the dam's sluice gates. Estuaries with a large difference in water level between high and low tide (the tidal range) are most suitable for barrages, for example:

- the Rance estuary barrage, Brittany, France
- the Bay of Fundy barrage, Eastern Canad
- the proposed Severn barrage across the Bristol Channel, South-West England.

Tidal power is a clean, predictable and renewable energy source but barrages do:

- reduce the use of an estuary for shipping and
- change its natural environment, especially for wildlife.

(See *renewable energy*.)

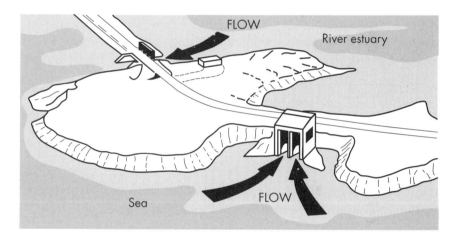

base flow: is part of the discharge of a river/stream. It is that part that is contributed by *groundwater* supplies. Groundwater seeps into the bed of the river at a fairly constant rate. During dry weather most or all of the discharge will be made up by base flow. *Hydrographs* can be drawn to show:

- base flow discharge and
- storm flow discharge.

base level: sea level for most rivers. This is the lowest level to which vertical erosion of a river's bed by running water can take place.

basic lava is molten rock from deep within the Earth. It is thin and fluid, flowing quickly and quietly over great distances before solidifying. Volcanoes formed from basic lava are known as shield volcanoes. Their long, gentle sides resemble a flattened shield. An example is Mauna Loa, Hawaii. (See *acid lava*.)

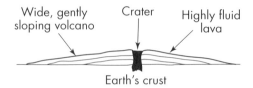

Wide, gently sloping volcano   Crater   Highly fluid lava

Earth's crust

battery farming is a type of animal farming. The animals, e.g. chickens, are reared:
- in small pens or cages along with many others
- indoors in a controlled environment
- with automatically delivered food and water
- quickly, having a short life.

An example of very intensive, commercial farming, it has lowered the price of meats and animal products but is opposed by some people, including animal rights groups and those concerned with food safety.

bay: a wide, deep indentation along a coastline i.e. where it makes a major swing in towards the land. On indented coasts where the coastline is not straight bays can occur together with capes or *headlands*. An example is the Purbeck coast, Dorset. Swanage and Studland Bays formed where the coast-line was worn back because the rocks were softer and less resistant to wave attack. Bay *beaches* are a frequently occurring type of beach.

beach: a depositional feature found along a coastline. Beach deposits are usually of sandy and pebbly materials deposited by the waves:
- where the beach is sheltered and the *waves* are low in energy and *constructive*
- where the supply of deposit materials is large.

Beaches form best on gently shelving coasts or at the protected back of a bay. In a bay, and in shallow water generally, friction slows down the waves. A flat-topped ridge towards the back of a beach at the highest point that the waves have reached is known as a berm.

Beaufort scale: a numerical scale for recording wind speed. The scale ranges from 0 to 12, and was devised by an Admiral Beaufort who related each number to wind effects upon visible features. Each number also has a descriptive term e.g. parts of Britain had *hurricane*-force winds (Force 12) during Christmas 1997. (See *anemometer*.)

Beaufort force	Descriptive term	Effects on visible features	Wind speed
0	Calm	Smoke rises vertically	0
1	Light air	Wind direction shown by smoke but not wind vanes	1–2
2	Light breeze	Wind felt on face; leaves rustle; wind vane moves to show the direction of wind	3–7
3	Gentle breeze	Leaves and twigs in constant motion Light flag extended	8–12
4	Moderate breeze	Dust and paper lifted Small branches move	13–17
5	Fresh breeze	Small trees in leaf begin to sway	18–22
6	Strong breeze	Large branches in motion; wind whistles in telegraph wire	23–27
Beaufort force	Descriptive term	Effects on visible features	Wind speed
7	Moderate gale	Dust and paper lifted Difficult to walk into the wind	13–17
8	Fresh gale	Twigs break off trees	33–37
9	Strong gale	Slight structural damage; slates and tiles blown off	38–47
10	Whole gale	Trees uprooted; considerable	48–55
11	Storm	Widespread damage Rare in Britain	56–63
12	Hurricane	Devastation	64 and over

bedding plane: the line which divides each layer or strata in sedimentary rock. This layer formation is a feature of sedimentary rocks. They formed from sediments, usually deposited under water. The point at which one period of deposition ended and another began is marked by a bedding plane. The bedding planes are generally clearly visible in shale and sandstones. They often make sedimentary rocks more vulnerable to weathering, as the rock can be attacked by the elements via its bedding planes.

bid-rent is the idea that those bidding the highest rent (i.e. price) for a piece of land will get the use of that land. The idea helps to explain land use patterns in towns and cities. High bid-rents (i.e. prices bid for land) in the towns and cities of *more economically developed countries* (MEDCs) today are found:

- in *central business districts* (CBDs) (i.e. town and city centres)
- on the *rural-urban fringe* because of their high *accessibilities*.

(See *peak land value intersection*.)

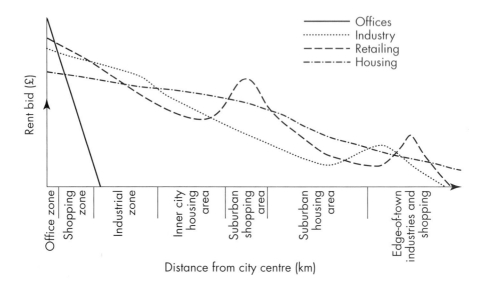

Distance from city centre (km)

biological weathering: takes place when plants and animals are involved in the *weathering* of rock. This involvement can take the form of:

- mechanical (or physical) weathering e.g. when tree roots shatter rocks by growing along their bedding planes
- chemical weathering e.g. soil bacteria and decomposing vegetation produce organic acids which speed up the chemical breakdown of rocks below.

(See *chemical weathering* and *mechanical weathering*.)

biomass: the amount of live (organic) matter, mainly vegetation in an area. In some countries biomass is a source of energy and chemicals. Alcohol extracted from plants such as sugar cane can be used to make PVC (a plastic), gasohol (a car fuel), and biogas (methane from rotting plant and animal waste). Half of the cars in Brazil run on gasohol.

birth rate: the number of live births per 1,000 people in a year. Generally, it is higher in *less economically developed countries* (LEDCs) than in *more economically developed countries* (MEDCs) e.g. in 1990 India had a birth rate of 27 and Sweden one of 11. Birth rate falls as a country develops economically because:

- family planning e.g. contraceptives, abortion is more widely available
- attitudes towards children and large families change e.g. women's' careers and material possessions, including holidays, become as important to people

as having children.
(See *demographic transition model*.)

bosnywash is the name given to the enormous urban area along the north east coast of the USA. This continuous urban area stretches from Boston in the north through New York to Washington in the south. It is an example of a megalopolis – a super-*conurbation* with a population of more than ten million people.

boulder clay is the unsorted material deposited by moving ice. It is:
- a mixture of various shapes and sizes of stones/boulders with sticky clay
- spread out in sheets to form a plain
- the result of earlier *erosion* by the ice – some of the stones/boulders in the boulder clays of East Yorkshire came from the Lake District; This boulder clay was deposited during the *Ice Age*
- also known as *till* or glacial drift.

braiding: takes place when a river splits from a single channel into several *channels*. It occurs most commonly in the lower course of a river, often on the *flood plain* where large-scale deposition of *alluvium* clogs its course and forces it to split into a network of channels. These channels are known as *distributaries*.

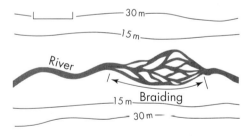

Brandt Report: this Report published in 1980, was named after its chairman, Herr Willy Brandt. It dealt with the fact that the world was divided economically between a 'rich North' (Northern Hemisphere) and a 'poor South' (Southern Hemisphere). However, it stressed that the two:
- are economically dependent upon each other (*interdependence*), and
- should trade freely with each other.
The world map showing the North–South divide that came out of the Report continues to form part of GCSE geography studies. Some small modifications to bring the details of the map up-to-date may be needed.

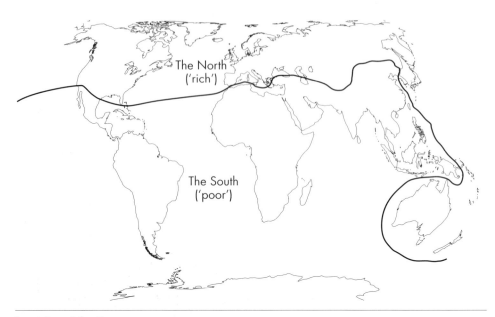

break of bulk is a place where cargo, e.g. raw materials, has to be unloaded because a new form of transport is to be used. Industries often locate at this point of unloading. Many port industries rely on the change of transport from sea to land. Locating the industries at the port e.g. steel from iron ore imported by sea and petro-chemicals from oil imported by sea tanker, saves some of the high costs of reloading the raw material.

bridge point is the place where a bridge has been or could be built across a river. This crossing point of the river develops into an important route centre and meeting place. Settlements usually develop at bridge points, especially lowest bridge points, the furthest point downstream that the river is bridged. Sea, river and road travel meet here. Newcastle developed at the lowest bridge point of the river Tyne.

brownfield site is a location, often for industry, on land which:
● was once used for industry and/or housing
● is now derelict
● may be polluted by industrial waste
● could be in an urban area, perhaps an *inner city* area.
Inner city redevelopment schemes are generally on brownfield sites. An example is the scheme to redevelop the former steel industry area in Sheffield's Lower Don Valley. The Meadowhall Shopping Centre, Sheffield Arena and the National Institute of Sport are on brownfield sites. (See *greenfield site* and *urban redevelopment*.)

business park: a location where businesses needing office accommodation can concentrate. They may be in a park setting and have leisure facilities such as a golf course. *High-tech industries* and *service* industries are attracted to business parks. (See *science/technology park*.)

Buys Ballots Law was named after its originator and describes the behaviour of the wind. His law is that if you stand with your back to the wind in the Northern Hemisphere low pressure will be to your left. Wind blows towards lower pressure but is bent to the right in the Northern Hemisphere by the Earth's rotation (known as the Coriolis Force). It is the exact opposite in the Southern Hemisphere.

calcification: the *deposition* of calcium in a *soil profile* due to weak leaching. It is a key process occurring in many of the worlds' soils. It helps to produce a group of soils called pedocals i.e. calcium/lime-accumulating soils such as a *chernozem*. It occurs in areas where:

- rainfall is too low to allow much percolation of water and dissolved minerals down through the soil
- evaporation is high causing dissolved calcium to rise through the soil before being deposited.

canopy: the high layer of vegetation in a woodland. In equatorial rainforests this layer of the crowns of tall trees can form an almost continuous cover preventing sunlight reaching the undergrowth below.

capital: the artificial resources used to produce goods and services. Equipment, machinery and computers, and the finance that has to be invested to make and use them, are all forms of capital.

capital-intensive refers to production which uses a lot of capital in relation to the other factors of production e.g. labour, knowledge. Agriculture and manufacturing industry are generally more capital-intensive in *more economically developed countries* (MEDCs) than in *less economically developed countries* (LEDCs). (See *factors of production* and *high-tech industry*.)

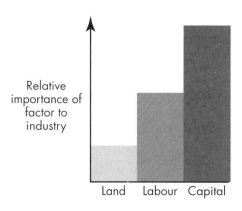

carboniferous limestone is a *sedimentary rock* and one of the types of limestone. It is:
- formed under water from the remains of living organisms
- a hard rock forming high ground (mountain limestone)
- pervious (i.e. has cracks and joints) and *permeable* (i.e. lets water through).

The White Peak area of the Derbyshire Pennines e.g. Matlock, Buxton and the Derbyshire Dales are carboniferous limestone. It forms very distinctive scenery known as *karst*.

cartography is the science and skill of making maps and charts.

cash crops are those grown for sale rather than for consumption by the farmer and family. Wheat grown in Britain for supermarket bread and coffee grown in Brazil are both examples of cash crops. Cash crops need a *market* and transport to that market, whether home or abroad. (See *commercial farming*.)

catchment area: the supply area for a river, or for a service such as a school or shopping centre. In the case of a river this area supplies water and is known as a *drainage basin*. The area supplying customers for a service is known as a *sphere of influence*.

cave: an underground hollow in the ground with an opening onto the Earth's surface. They are most commonly found:
- along a rocky coastline, especially on *headlands* – weaker areas of rock are eroded by the waves; *hydraulic action* is important in the growth of the cave by further erosion
- in limestone regions where acidic rainwater dissolves areas of the rock underground.

(See *wave refraction* for sea caves and *karst scenery* and *corrosion* for limestone caves.)

census: the massive data collection exercise to measure the size and nature of the population; it occurs in Britain once every ten years. Every household has to complete a form on a set date; the last census was on 21 April 1991. Completed forms give information about the people and amenities in that household.

central business district (CBD): the major shopping and commercial area of a town or city. It is commonly known as the town or city centre and has the following features.

- A central and highly accessible position. Roads from all over the town/city usually meet at this location.
- Close to or around the original site and old core of the town/city e.g. bridge, cathedral.
- A great range and choice of goods and services for sale, including *high order goods* e.g. fashion clothing and specialist services e.g. accountancies.
- High land values. Rents are expensive because of the *accessibility* and prestige of the location.
- A small residential population. People work and shop rather than live here.
- Large numbers of pedestrians during the day when it is the busiest place in the town/city.
- Multi-storey buildings and a high intensity of building. The tallest buildings are usually found in the CBD.
- Clustering of similar businesses e.g. comparison goods such as shoe shops, and specialist services such as legal firms.
- A core area including the most important shops e.g. Marks & Spencer and the busiest point (e.g. the *peak land value intersection*) and a frame area of car parks, bus and rail stations, offices, hotels, etc.
- Traffic congestion or measures to avoid congestion e.g. one-way streets, pedestrian walkways.

(See *ordinary business district* (OBD) and *comparison goods*.)

chalk: a permeable *sedimentary rock* forming much of the landscape of southern England. It is a very pure form of limestone, white and rather soft. Chalk landscape is distinctive and consists of:
- little or no surface drainage – chalk is porous and so *permeable*
- dry valleys which once contained rivers
- low rounded hills, called downs in southern England
- escarpments where the chalk outcrop is dipped
- short grassland with occasional woodland.

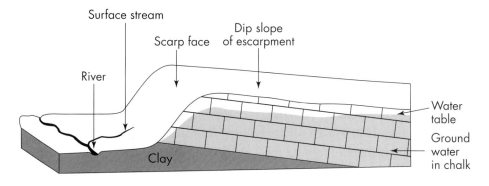

The North Downs of Kent and the South Downs of Sussex are examples of chalk landscapes.

channel: the trough between two banks in which stream or river's water flows. Stream/river channels have banks and a bed. The term can also be used to describe a narrow stretch of sea between two land areas which connects two larger sea areas e.g. the English Channel, and the deeper part of a bay or harbour which is navigable for shipping.

chemical weathering: the break up of rocks due to exposure to the chemicals in air and water. These chemicals can react with some minerals in some rocks. Affected rocks may:
- dissolve in water e.g. a limestone solution occurs because the carbon dioxide in rainwater makes a weak carbonic acid (carbonation)
- oxidise e.g. iron turns into iron oxide in the presence of oxygen and leads to the rock's collapse
- break down into clay due to a reaction with hydrogen in water e.g. hydrolysis causes the breakdown of granite.

Chemical weathering occurs at a faster rate:
- in hot, wet conditions e.g. the Tropics
- on rocks with certain minerals e.g. calcium carbonate
- where rainwater is more acidic because of organic acid from decaying vegetation or atmospheric pollution (i.e. acid rain).

(See *weathering*.)

chernozem is grassland soil. It develops on dry temperate continental grasslands e.g. the steppes of Ukraine. Chernozem soils are:
- rich, deep soils ideal for farming
- also known as black earths because of the colour of their A-horizon
- subjected to only minor leaching (i.e. melting spring snow) due to the dry climate and some uplift of water and minerals through the soil.

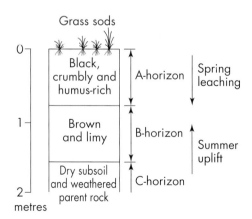

chloropleth: a map which uses colour-shading, line-shading or stippling to show a geographical distribution e.g. a world map showing the distribution of population over the Earth. Understanding the key is vital to reading a chloropleth.

cliff recession is the process by which cliffs move back from their previous position. Cliffs are sloping rock surfaces along a coastline. They are eroded by:
- the cliff face being attacked by wind, rain etc.
- the cliff foot being attacked by waves.
Debris is removed by the sea and the cliff retreats landward. The shape of a cliff depends upon various factors, including the type of rock it is made of. (See *destructive waves*, *erosion* and *headland*.)

climate: a summary of all the changes, say from day to day in an area's *weather*. The summary is usually presented as tables and charts of averages for rainfall, temperature and other weather elements. Climate is derived from weather observations. Its function is to describe the overall nature of the weather to be expected in a particular area. (See *climatograph*.)

climatic change: the idea that the climate of an area does change over time and that changes have occurred in the past and may be doing so at present. For example, over the last three million years Britain has experienced many changes of climate, including:
- cold glacial periods during the *Ice Age*, and
- a cooler period called the Little Ice Age between the 14th and 19th centuries.
The *global warming* we seem to be experiencing at present is an example of a climatic change. What might happen to climate in the future is still not certain but any global warming is thought to be the result of human actions which pollute the atmosphere. The causes of natural changes of climate in the past are very uncertain.

climatic region: a large area of the Earth experiencing a broadly similar *climate*. There are around a dozen of these regions in three types of area:
- tropical areas e.g. the Equatorial climatic region with its hot, wet climate
- temperate areas e.g. the Mediterranean (or warm western temperate) climatic region – this region includes the lands around the Mediterranean as well as areas of Australia, New Zealand, South Africa, South America and California
- polar areas e.g. the tundra climatic region.
Britain lies in the same cool western temperate region as southern Chile and the South Island of New Zealand. (See *climatograph*.)

climatograph: a graph showing the average monthly values for temperature and rainfall at a place. These values are plotted on the graph as:
- a line for temperature
- vertical bars for rainfall.

The *climate* of any *climatic region* can be shown as a climatograph for a chosen location within that region.

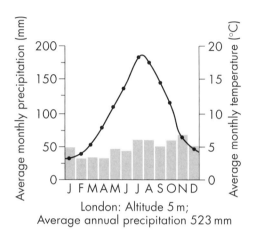

London: Altitude 5 m;
Average annual precipitation 523 mm

climax vegetation is a plant community ideally suited to its environment i.e. soil and climate. The vegetation of an area normally takes time to reach its climax type but, once it does, it will not change as long as the environment remains unchanged. Oak woodland is considered to be the climax vegetation on the lowlands of central England (the Midlands).

clouds are masses of minute water droplets and/or ice crystals visible in the sky. They are formed when a large body of air cools to its *dewpoint* and the water vapour condenses into cloud. Each type of cloud has its own shape and height, for instance:
- cirrus are high, wispy clouds
- stratus are layer clouds
- cumulus are billowy, puffy clouds.

Clouds are very important in influencing the weather and climate we experience, for instance:
- they block out incoming radiation from the Sun
- they trap in the atmosphere radiation outgoing from the Earth
- rain falls from some of them.

Clouds are good indicators of the weather we are getting or about to get, for instance:

- cirrus indicates a depression on the way
- alto-cumulus is associated with dry, warm weather.

(See *condensation* and *depression*.)

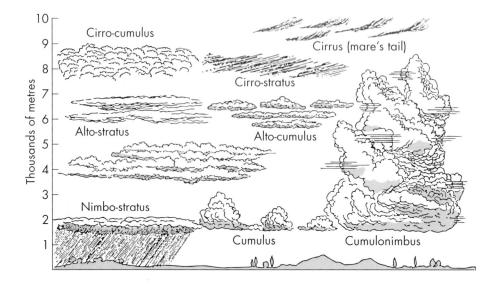

coastline: the narrow stretch of land which borders the sea. It includes the top of any cliffs as well as the shoreline where land and sea actually meet. The shoreline is under the direct influence of the waves. The coastline is where wave and land processes interact.

cold front: the boundary between a mass of advancing cold air and stationary warm air. At the Earth's surface the denser cold air pushes underneath the lighter warm air in front of it. The warm air rising above the wedge of cold air leads to cloud formation. The weather associated with the overhead passage of a cold *front* includes:

- a heavy rain shower
- a drop in temperature
- the wind increasing speed and changing direction
- dark cumulo-nimbus clouds and perhaps thunder.

The front can be several hundred kilometres wide and the final front in the passage of a *depression*.)

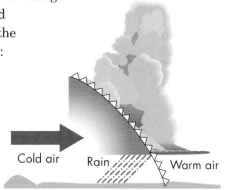

collective farming: an arrangement in which government land is farmed by a group who work together sharing resources, production and profits. Collective farms tend to be large but operate as a single unit. A Chinese commune, which is typically about 5,000 hectares in size, is an example of collective farming. They:
- are self-governing
- pay rent for the land and part of their profits to the government
- receive production targets from the government.

commercial farming: the growing of crops and/or rearing of livestock for sale in the market. Practically all farming in *more economically developed countries* (MEDCs) is commercial. The intention is to maximise yields and profits. (See *agribusiness* and *cash crops*.)

Common Agricultural Policy (CAP): the scheme for organising agriculture in the European Union countries. It involves:
- trying to guarantee food supplies by making farming efficient
- trying to keep food prices reasonable
- trying to keep jobs and fair incomes for farmers.

This is mainly achieved through the fixing of prices by the scheme. Regardless of whether there is too much or too little food produced farmers are guaranteed a set price per unit. Shoppers have had stable food supplies and prices and farmers therefore jobs and a good income, but too much food has been produced as a result. All the overproduction not needed in the shops was bought up by the European Union at great cost and stored at further cost. The method of reducing these food surpluses e.g. butter mountains and wine lakes, are the quotas set by the European Union. Any farmer found going over a quota, or top production limit, is fined.

A fuller picture of the workings of the CAP is shown by the cartoon below e.g. loans and grants to farmers to enable them to buy new equipment or encourage them to improve land or grow certain crops.

Some advantages of the Common Agricultural Policy are as follows.
- The European Union is now largely self-sufficient in food.
- Farming is very productive.
- Almost all farmers, even those farming more difficult environments have been able to stay in business.

Some disadvantages of the scheme are as follows.
- It is very bureaucratic (i.e. paper and officials).
- It is open to fiddling and abuse.
- It has kept food prices higher than they might have been.

- Farmers in more inefficient farming areas e.g. France and southern Europe are favoured at the expense of those in more efficient farming areas e.g. Britain.

commune: a large unit of land which is owned and managed by the community living on it. These units are a feature of communism in rural China and involve cooperation, communal living and *collective farming*. Private ownership and work has developed on the communes of modern China. Communes can be at least 100 sq km in size and are responsible for local government e.g. schools, health and public hygiene as well as farming.

commuting: the daily movement of people between a settlement in which they live and another in which they work. Modern transport facilities mean that people no longer need to live where they work. These daily journeys to and from work can be between:
- two urban settlements e.g. living in Brighton and travelling the 120 mile return journey every day to work in London
- a rural settlement and an urban settlement e.g. the village of Hathersage in the Derbyshire Peak District is a commuter village for many people working 12 miles away in Sheffield i.e. Hathersage lies within Sheffield's commuter belt.

All urban settlements have a commuter belt around them from which people travel to work. The dormitory towns of Dorking and Reigate in Surrey lie within London's commuter belt. (See *dormitory settlements*.)

comparison goods are goods which compete with other makes of the product and which people normally choose to buy after making comparisons. They are usually:
- *high-order* goods which people buy occasionally e.g. shoes, jewellery
- sold in comparison shops which specialise in that product and are found close to each other in the town/city centre e.g. shoe shops often cluster in the *central business district* to enable shoppers to make comparisons before buying.

(See *convenience goods*.)

composite volcano: a *volcano* made up of alternate layers of lava, ash and any other ejected materials. These are the highest and most common volcanoes, and have been built up by several eruptions. Mt Vesuvius in Italy, Mt Fuji in Japan and Mt Popacatapetl in Mexico are examples.

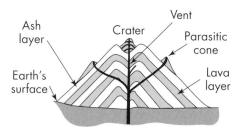

compression is the name of the force which drives different parts of the Earth's crust towards each other. This force folds and bends and so shortens the crust. Upfolds known as anticlines, downfolds known as synclines, and *fold mountains* such as the Alps are all produced by compression. (See *folding*.)

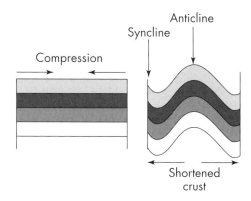

concentric models are diagrams which generalise and simplify land use in the real world by showing it as rings around a centre. These ring diagrams are used in both urban and agricultural geography. The concentric urban model shows:
- a *central business district* (CBD)
- how the town/city has grown outwards like a tree from its old centre
- how different socio-economic groups of people segregate and occupy certain areas.
- industry only as part of the transition zone in the inner city
- a zone of villages (zone 5) from which people *commute* to work in the town/city.

The concentric agricultural model suggests that farmers use their land differently according to how near or far they are from a large town/city (market). Close to this market they may concentrate on more bulky, perishable products such as milk and vegetables. Further away, increased *extensive farming* of more valuable products such as meat may take place. (See *socio-economic*.)

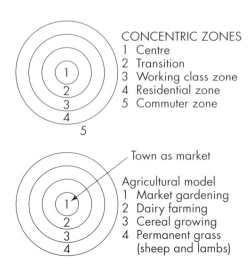

CONCENTRIC ZONES
1 Centre
2 Transition
3 Working class zone
4 Residential zone
5 Commuter zone

Town as market

Agricultural model
1 Market gardening
2 Dairy farming
3 Cereal growing
4 Permanent grass
  (sheep and lambs)

condensation is the process by which water vapour forms into tiny droplets of water. This happens when the air carrying the water vapour cools down and its temperature falls to its *dewpoint*. *Clouds* are formed by condensation.

conflict of interest: the clash of opinion between different groups of people over the use of a resource, often land. Conflicts are part of the study of the great geographical issues of today's world. For example, should farmland be used for house-building ? Should we slow down the rate of intensification of agriculture and car use? Any decisions involve considering the views of various groups of people.

confluence: the meeting point of two or more stream or river *channels*. For example, the confluence of the rivers Thames and Isis is where the two channels unite at Oxford. (See *drainage basin*.)

conservation: the maintenance and protection of resources and environments. Maintaining both for future use is vital if, for example, the resource is in increasingly short supply e.g. North Sea fish or the environment is fragile and threatened by peoples' activities e.g. coral reefs. Conservation includes:
- work to renovate buildings of historic interest
- recognising sites of special scientific interest to protect an ecosystem
- slowing down the use of non-renewable resources e.g. oil
- recycling of resources, especially non-renewable ones e.g. paper, aluminium cans
- laws affecting land use in an area e.g. National Parks, Green Belts.

conservative plate boundary: the place where two plates forming the Earth's crust meet but at which land is neither created nor lost. The plates move past each other parallel to the boundary. This can be either:

- in opposite directions or
- in the same direction but at different speeds e.g. as along the San Andreas Fault – the conservative plate boundary in California.

Earthquakes can occur along conservative plate boundaries, especially when pressure builds up after the two plates lock together rather than slide smoothly past each other. (See *plate tectonics*.)

constructive plate boundary: the place where two plates move away from each other. Molten material rises to fill the gap and so new crust is formed. An example is the Mid-Atlantic Ridge on the bed of the Atlantic Ocean. This ocean floor is growing as the new crust is formed. Volcanic islands such as Iceland mark the high point of the mostly underwater ridge. (See *destructive plate boundaries, plate tectonics, divergent plate boundaries* and *volcanoes*.)

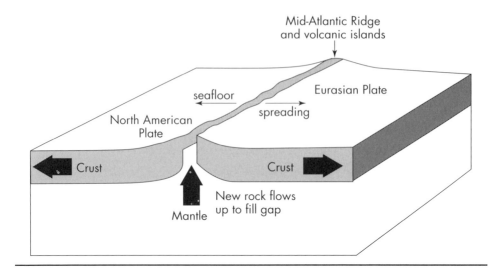

constructive waves cause material to accumulate on a shore. There will be more deposition than erosion so beaches will grow. They are low waves with a longer wavelength, and break about every ten seconds. This means that:

- the *swash* is stronger and surges far up the shoreline carrying material with it
- the *backwash* is gentle so little material is removed.

They form flat, large beaches. They are also known as swash waves or surging breakers.

continentality refers to the climate of a place which is affected more by land than by the influence of the water in the sea. Climates deep in the centre of continents have:

- warm/hot summers
- cold winters
- a large annual temperature range (i.e. the difference between summer and winter)
- low rainfall with most in the summer.

These are explained by the great distance from the sea of places like central Russia:

- moist sea winds rarely reach these places
- land and sea also heat up and cool down at different rates: land heats up and cools down more rapidly than water; land is the warmer in summer but the cooler in winter.

In Britain, Kent has a more continental climate than Cornwall; Kent is nearer the continent of Europe and Cornwall is surrounded by the Atlantic Ocean. (See *oceanic climate*.)

continental plate: a tectonic plate made of rocks which form a large area of land. These are the older, lighter and thicker rocks which rest on oceanic crust below and form the continents. The South American Plate is an example. (See *convergent plate boundary*, *destructive plate boundary* and *plate tectonics*.)

contour: a line drawn on an Ordnance Survey map through points which are at the same height above sea level. They can be used to provide map information about:
- the height (altitude) of places
- the general shape of the ground i.e. its relief, including specific landforms e.g. valleys, plateaux
- the steepness of sloping ground i.e. its gradient.
On an Ordnance Survey map with a 1:50,000 scale contours are marked every ten metres; this is known as the contour interval.

contour ploughing is a farming method which reduces soil *erosion* on sloping farmland. The land is ploughed at right angles to the slope, following its natural contours. This forms ridges and furrows along the slope which check the downhill flow of rainwater. Rain infiltrates into the ground rather than forming gullies up and down the slope. Gully erosion is a major type of *soil erosion*.

contract farming: takes place where farmers and *agribusinesses* work to production contracts they have signed with large supermarkets or food companies. Roughly half of British food is produced under contract, for instance:
- large supermarkets generally have contracts with farmers/farming companies to supply them with pork and poultry
- large food companies e.g. Birdseye (Unilever) often have contracts with farmers to supply them with vegetables for freezing or canning.

conurbation: a large and almost continuous built-up area:
- with a population of at least one million
- where a number of towns/cities have grown into each other.
Urban sprawl within a town/city leads to it merging into others. The city of Sheffield and the towns of Doncaster, Rotherham and Barnsley have sprawled outwards to form the South Yorkshire conurbation. (See p 34 and *megalopolis*.)

convection: the rising of air, water or other materials because they have been heated and are warmer than their surroundings. Warm air rises, for example, because it becomes lighter than surrounding colder air.

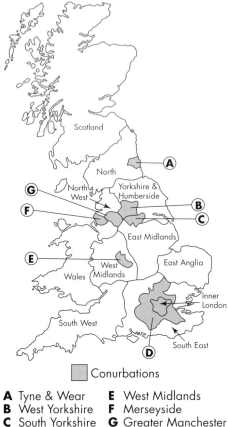

Conurbations

Conurbation

A Tyne & Wear   **E** West Midlands
B West Yorkshire   **F** Merseyside
C South Yorkshire   **G** Greater Manchester
D Greater London

convectional rain is that which falls from clouds produced by convection currents. They form when:

- warm air rises from a hot land surface e.g. during a summer heatwave in Britain
- cold air crosses a warm sea e.g. northerly winds crossing the Mediterranean in autumn.

Cumulo-nimbus (thick, billowy and dark) clouds and thunderstorms are associated with convectional rain.

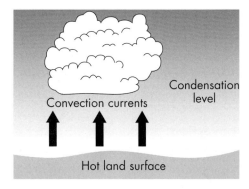

convenience goods are goods which are bought frequently, often daily. These *low-order*, everyday items such as bread, milk and newspapers need to be conveniently available for people. Convenience shops are located in various parts of a town/city. People do not generally travel any great distance to shop for convenience goods.

convergent plate boundary is another name for a *destructive plate boundary*. Land is destroyed where plates converge.

cooperative farming is when individual farmers agree to organise their farming so as to cooperate with other farmers. They can cooperate both for buying inputs, such as seeds, or for selling their products. Cooperative farming is well-developed in Denmark. Cooperation has meant that farmers with small farms can benefit from the advantages of a large-scale organisation by:
- buying cheaper inputs because of bulk buying
- pooling their resources of knowledge and equipment
- sharing costs of packaging, transport etc.
- negotiating better prices for *contract farming*.

core and periphery: areas with vastly different levels of economic development. Development and wealth are never evenly spread. In core areas of a country or larger area e.g. the whole world wealth, population and resources are concentrated. Areas less developed and less populated than the core are known as periphery areas. For example:
- within Britain South-East England in and around London is regarded as a core area whereas Cornwall is considered to be a periphery area
- on a world scale the *more economically developed countries* (MEDCs) of the Northern Hemisphere are core areas with the *less economically developed countries* (LRDCs) of the South periphery areas.

The core and periphery areas of part of Europe are shown on the map below.

corrasion: another name for *abrasion*. Any material carried by rivers, the sea, ice or the wind rubs against the ground and helps to slowly wear it away.

corrie: a steep-sided hollow high on a mountain side like an horse-shoe-shaped armchair. It marks the source of a former glacier and today may have a small lake in it. There are numerous corries in the English Lake District, which are known as cwms in Wales and cirques in the French Alps. Small hollows were turned into deep corries as the ice accumulated and eroded the rocks. Ice eventually moved out of the corrie and started its journey down-valley as a glacier. Corries are remains of an ice age. (See *glaciation*.)

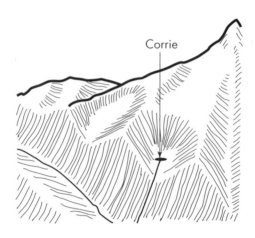

corrosion: the *solution* of certain minerals in rocks when they come into contact with water. This is *chemical weathering* with removal of the dissolved material, that is, an erosional process. Calcium carbonate in limestones is easily dissolved and removed in solution by rivers and the sea.

cottage industry: when people work in their own homes, often using their own equipment, to produce goods for sale. Cottage workers may be employees and their products collected regularly by their employer. Some clothes production in India is organised as a cottage industry. Homeworking is cottage industry.

counterurbanisation: the movement of population away from large urban areas. It is the opposite process to *urbanisation* and has been occurring in most *more economically developed countries* (MEDCs), including Britain in recent times. Britain's population has become less concentrated in its large cities; London, Manchester and Liverpool, for example, have all lost population since 1961. Smaller towns and rural areas have gained population in this migration. Reasons for the migration include:
- people feeling 'pushed' out of urban areas with their problems of crime, decay and pollution
- people feeling 'pulled' into more rural areas by the so-called 'charm of the countryside lifestyle'
- improvements in public e.g. high-speed trains and private (car) transport meaning long-distance commuting is now possible
- new ways of working e.g. by computer from home and new locations for industry e.g. greenfield sites by motorways near small market towns.

(See *urban-to-rural migration* and *push and pull factors*.)

crater: the hole at the top of a volcanic cone. It is usually a circular hollow at the top of the *volcano*'s opening to the air or vent. Eruptions from the vent form the crater and its rim.

crust: the solid outside layer of the Earth. Here molten material has cooled to form solid rock. The crust:
- is divided into a series of large slabs known as tectonic plates which float on the molten interior of the Earth
- forms the sea bed and the continents
- is very unstable in places – crustal instability is greatest at the boundaries of the tectonic plates where the crust can be growing, shrinking or subject to earthquake.

(See *plate tectonics*.)

cycles of decline or growth show how an area can become either more and more run-down or more and more wealthy and successful economically as time goes by. Declining areas get trapped in a vicious circle, or downward spiral, whereas a virtuous circle, or upward spiral, sets up in growing areas. Breaking these circles/spirals can take time.

Cycle of decline

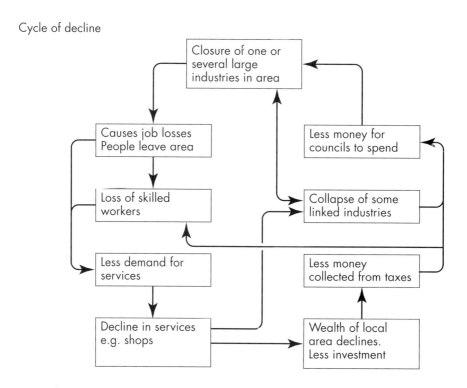

Cycle of growth

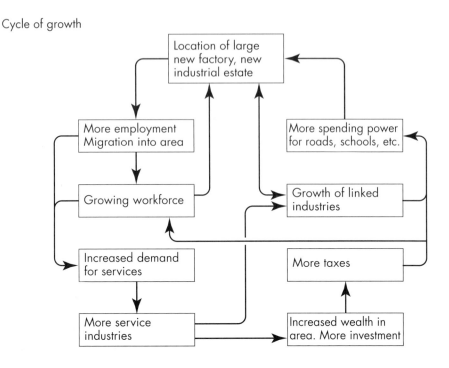

cycle of poverty (deprivation) is a vicious circle in which people in poorer areas can become trapped. It may operate in:
- rural areas, especially in *less economically developed countries* (LEDCs)
- the most deprived inner city areas in *more economically developed countries* (MEDCs) which can become urban ghettoes when the inhabitants become persistently trapped in this vicious downward spiral.

A cycle of rural poverty which may occur amongst farmers in LEDCs as shown below. (See *cycles of decline or growth*.)

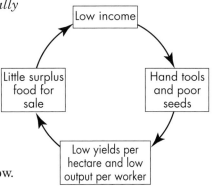

---

cyclone: a low air pressure area in the West Pacific e.g. China, Japan or the Philippines which brings severe weather similar to a *hurricane* and is characterised by:
- strong winds
- heavy rain.

dairy farming: concerned with the rearing of cattle for their milk. It is *intensive* farming and often found close to:

- populated urban areas
- rapid transport facilities e.g. motorways, railways.

Farming areas specialising in dairy cattle may not need such quick access to large urban markets if they use the milk to produce other dairy products e.g. cheese, yoghurt.

death rate: the number of deaths per 1000 people in a year. Generally, it is higher in *less economically developed countries* (LEDCs) than in *more economically developed countries* (MEDCs) e.g. in 1994 Sierra Leone had a death rate of 25 and Britain one of 11. The difference can be explained by differences in:

- medical provision
- hygiene and sanitation
- diet.

War or peace also have a significant influence on the death rate. (See *demographic transition model*.)

debris: fragments of loose material produced as rocks *weather*. Debris varies in size from small boulders to fine sand. The scree slopes of the limestone areas of the Pennines are an example. Debris can accumulate in one place and some is transported from where it was formed.

debt: money owed to others, perhaps in the case of *less economically developed countries* (LEDCs) to governments, banks or companies in other countries. Many of these countries, especially those in Africa and South America have a growing international debt problem. Argentina, for example, had an international debt of 65 billion dollars in 1994 which was roughly six times its annual earnings from exports. Meeting the interest payments alone on this sort of debt is at best a struggle and often impossible for LEDCs. Many have a debt crisis which increases poverty in the country and hinders its development. Ways of reducing the debt without harming living standards and development need to be found.

decentralisation: the movement of population or industry away from an established central location around which it has become concentrated. The re-location of many government offices out of central locations in London is an example of decentralisation e.g. the Accounts General Department of the Post Office to Chesterfield and the Vehicle Licensing Department to Swansea. Decentralisation involves movement from a *core* area towards a *periphery* area. (See *deglomeration*.)

deflation: the blowing away of small, loose materials such as sand by the wind. It can occur:
- in sandy deserts
- on sandy shorelines, especially where there are sand dunes.

Small hollows and blow outs are frequently left in these areas after a period of deflation.

deforestation: the deliberate clearing of forest. Large numbers of trees are cut or burned down in the *tropical rainforests*:
- in order that the land can be used for other purposes e.g. farming or road building
- to produce timber.

Deforestation e.g. in Amazonia and Indonesia has serious environmental effects, both locally and worldwide. There are great efforts to slow down the pace of deforestation in many tropical areas.

deglomeration is the opposite of *agglomeration*. It is the movement of firms away from areas in which they were once concentrated (agglomerated). British newspaper production was once concentrated in Fleet Street, London; it is now much more dispersed having deglomerated because of high costs of land, labour and transport in Fleet Street. (See *decentralisation*.)

de-industrialisation: the shrinking of a country's manufacturing (secondary) sector of industry. Britain has been de-industrialising since the 1970s and now employs fewer manufacturing workers and produces less manufacturing output than in 1970. Areas which relied on traditional heavy manufacturing industry e.g. Sheffield and its steelworks in the Lower Don Valley, have experienced unemployment and decline. De-industrialisation is de-manufacturing only and can result in an area swinging into new service industries to replace the old manufacturing industries as in Sheffield's Lower Don Valley. (See *tertiarisation*.)

delta: a low-lying area of *alluvium* at the mouth of a river, most likely to occur where the river:
- carries a large load
- enters a sea or lake with weak tides and currents.

A river will deposit more alluvium than the tides and currents can remove. Large rivers like the Nile and Rhone have built deltas in the relatively tideless Mediterranean Sea. Deltas extend the land into the sea and vary in size and shape.

---

demographic transition model: a graph showing the four stages through which the populations of countries have generally passed as a result of natural changes – i.e. births and deaths. Natural increase in population occurs as shown in Stages 2 and 3 when births exceed deaths. Stages 1 and 4 are periods of little or no change in the size of the natural population; births and deaths balance each other out. *More economically developed countries* (MEDCs) tend to be in Stage 4 at present; many *less economically developed countries* (LEDCs) in Stages 2 or 3. (See *birth rate* and *death rate*.)

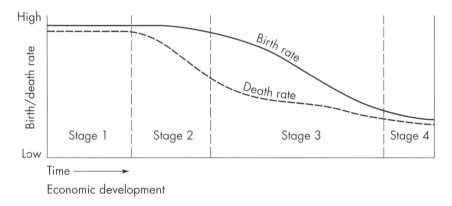

---

dendritic: this term describes a drainage pattern of river and stream *channels* in the shape of tree roots. This tree-like appearance develops where rocks are the same or show equal resistance to *erosion* over an area.

Tributaries called insequent streams

Main channel called consequent stream

density of population: the number of people per square kilometre. It enables regions and countries of different size to be compared fairly e.g. China with its large population but large area with Holland and its small area and population. Using the formula:

$$\text{Population density} = \frac{\text{Population}}{\text{Area}}$$

Holland is the more densely populated with a density of 339. China has a density of 89. Densities are plotted on maps to show *population distributions*.

---

dependency ratio: the proportion of a country's population which is of working age (i.e. 15–65) in relation to the proportion which is of non-working age (i.e. under 15 and over 65).

● The ratio in most *more economically developed countries* (MEDCs) is between 50 and 70 but is likely to worsen as rising *life expectancy* increases the number of elderly dependants. In Britain in 1990 there were 52 people dependant upon every 100 working age people.
● The ratio in some *less economically developed countries* (LEDCs) is over 100 because of their high *birth rate* and large numbers of young dependants.

---

deposition: the laying down or dumping of sediments to form new features and landforms. Deposited sediments have previously been weathered and transported by running water, ice, wind, the sea or *mass movement. Deltas, moraines, beaches, spits* and sand dunes are all examples of depositional *landforms. Sedimentary* rocks were also once the result of deposition, often on the bed of a sea.

---

depression: a temporary, moving cell of below average air pressure in the westerly winds in *temperate* latitudes.

● Pressure is low in the centre and increases towards the outside.
● *Isobars* form an oval or circular shape.
● Winds blow in towards the centre anticlockwise in the Northern Hemisphere and clockwise in the Southern Hemisphere.
● *Cloud* and rain are formed at the two *fronts* in the depression. Warm front rain from low, thick cloud is light, steady and continuous. The later cold front rain from very thick, towering cloud is heavy but for a short period.
Occluded depressions in which the warm and cold fronts have joined show that it is beginning to fill in and die.

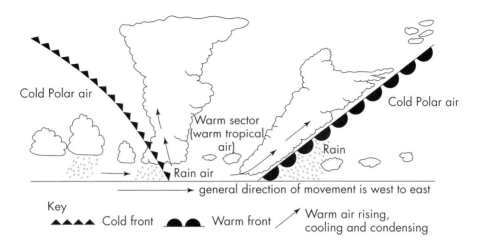

A cross-section through a depression showing the weather
experienced during its passage overhead.

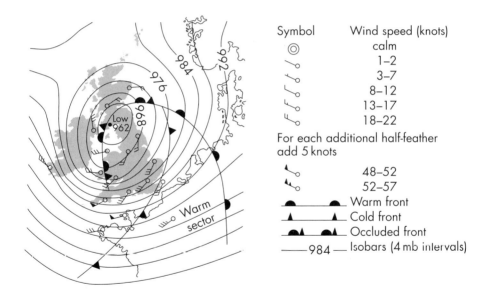

Symbol	Wind speed (knots)
◎	calm
	1–2
	3–7
	8–12
	13–17
	18–22

For each additional half-feather
add 5 knots

	48–52
	52–57
●———●	Warm front
▲———▲	Cold front
▲●———▲●	Occluded front
———984—	Isobars (4 mb intervals)

A depression as shown on a weather map

deprivation: a measure of how poor or badly off people are. Deprived people
are at a disadvantage in relation to others. Their well-being is below what is
perceived as reasonable for the country at the time because some or all of the
following needs are not met:
- the need for income (state benefits are being claimed)
- the need for a job (they are unemployed)

- the need for decent housing e.g. people may lack amenities such as central heating or live in overcrowded conditions
- for social support e.g. single parents.

Characteristics

- Deprivation is often multiple – people being unemployed, being unhealthy, on low income, having no car and no holiday.
- Deprivation is often cyclical – a cycle of deprivation can transmit relative poverty from one generation to the next and make escape from deprivation difficult.
- Deprivation is to be found in both urban and rural areas. Run-down property in inner city areas may be a sign of urban deprivation. Households in rural areas without a car may be disadvantaged because services and jobs are not accessible for them. Rural deprivation exists in many of the more remote rural areas of Britain e.g. Central Wales. (See *relative poverty*.)

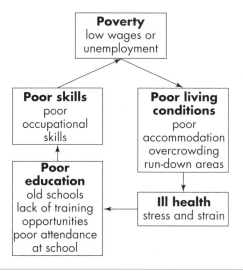

desalination: the removal of salt from seawater to make it suitable for human use. Desalination plants are found:

- in those parts of the world desperately short of water, especially desert areas
- along coastlines
- in *more economically developed countries* (MEDCs) rather than *less economically developed countries* (LEDCs) because the process is a costly one.

  Desalinated water is far more expensive than reservoir, river or well water. There are desalination plants on the western shore of the Persian Gulf in Saudi Arabia and Kuwait.

desertification: the spread of a desert into a neighbouring area. This area must have previously received enough rain not to be desert and support an almost continuous plant cover. The Sahara desert has been gradually advancing southwards into the area known as the Sahel. This was an area which was partly desert and partly savanna grassland. The causes of desertification are both:

- climatic i.e. reduced rainfall and
- human e.g. falling death rates leading to population growth and rising demand for food causing overgrazing of pastures.

In the Sahel e.g. Ethiopia and Sudan, famine and population migrations have occurred.

desire line: a line drawn on a map to show the *range* of a good or service. This range is the furthest distance from home that a person is willing to travel in order to obtain that good or service. Desire lines are used to work out *spheres of influence*.

destructive plate boundary: a place where two plates move towards each other. They converge or collide. This happens off the west coast of South America. The lighter oceanic crust of the Nazca plate dips downwards into the Earth's molten mantle beneath the heavier continental plate forming South America. The oceanic crust sinks, melts and is destroyed. This is called *subduction*. Collision and subduction lead to the formation of:

- *ocean trenches*
- *fold mountains*
- *earthquakes*
- *volcanoes*.

(See *convergent plate boundary* and *plate tectonics*.)

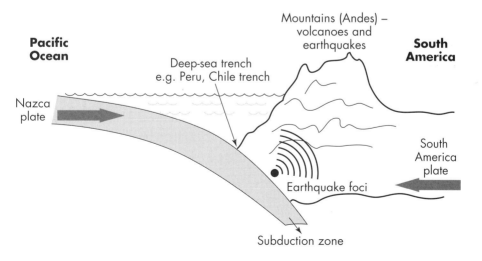

destructive waves move material down a *beach* towards the sea. They are short, steep waves which break about every four seconds. This means that:
- the *swash* is gentle and does not go far up the beach as the wave breaks almost vertically
- the *backwash* is strong and removes material from the beach.

They form short, steep beaches. They are also known as backwash waves or plunging/surfing breakers.

development usually means economic development or growing *wealth* in an area. This normally brings with it human development for most of the population. Growing wealth provides the means to pay for an improvement in people's *welfare* and *quality of life*. Countries with higher levels of economic development i.e. *more economically developed countries* (MEDCs) have usually managed to develop both material living standards and quality of life for most of their people. Most of the population of *less economically developed countries* (LEDCs) have lower material living standards and quality of life because economic development has been slower. There are various indicators of development in use. For example:
- *gross domestic/gross national product* (GNP, GDP) per person
- *life expectancy*
- *infant mortality rate*
- *literacy rate*
- number of cars per 1,000 people.

(See *standard of living*.)

development area is a region in need of development. They are also known as Assisted Areas because government tries to assist their development by offering industries incentives to locate in that region. Industries locating in these regions in Britain receive grants from the British Government and the European Union's Regional Development Fund. Regions may be in need of development because:
- they have never experienced much economic growth e.g. southern Italy
- they have experienced economic decline as old industries have died e.g. Merseyside.

(See *core and periphery* and *regional policy*.)

development gap: the difference between the economic development of the *more economically developed countries* (MEDCs), mainly in the Northern Hemisphere and that of the *less economically developed countries* (LEDCs), mainly in the Southern Hemisphere. This North–South gap, which may be widening, was highlighted by the *Brandt Report.*

dew is the moisture left on plants, leaves and the ground after water vapour in the air has cooled and condensed. The temperature at which this *condensation* occurs is known as the *dewpoint*. Dew forms most readily during a clear, calm night following a warm day. The moisture in the air picked up during the warm day will condense out as dew as the air cools down to its dewpoint during the night. (See *anticyclone*.)

dewpoint: the temperature at which the condensation of water vapour in the air occurs, causing dew. At this temperature the air has become saturated i.e. relative humidity is 100%.

discharge: the quantity of water passing through a river or stream channel's cross-section at a certain point. It is measured in cumecs (i.e. cubic metres per second) as follows:

area of cross-section (width × depth of channel) × velocity of water

dispersed settlement: where there is a scatter of individual farms, isolated dwellings and other small settlements across an area e.g. the hamlets and isolated farms of the Scottish Highlands and Islands. Pastoral farming, poorly developed transport and communications, and more challenging physical environments can be linked with a dispersed settlement pattern.

distance-decay: the principle that distance reduces influence. The amount of interaction between two places or two people is likely to decrease as the distance between them increases. It may be the case that the further away a place is the less you know about it. Improvements in transport and communications have modified the distance-decay (or friction of distance) principle.

distributary: a small river *channel* which has left a larger, main channel. On a *delta* rivers usually *braid* or split into numerous distributaries.

distribution has two meanings in geography:
- the way in which a feature is spread across an area to produce a pattern which will show up on a map e.g. the distribution of *volcanoes* in the world or of open space within a city
- the process of getting products from the producer to the consumer e.g. how eggs are transported from farms into homes.

divergent plate boundary is another name for a *constructive plate boundary*. Where plates diverge new land is created by rising lava/magma.

diversification: when a business decides to move into other product(s) and/or market(s). It is a way of:

- growing e.g. Marks & Spencer diversified when they added financial services to their business activities
- surviving e.g. with farm incomes falling in many parts of the European Union some farmers have developed other business interests such as bed-and-breakfast, forestry.

dormant: used to describe a *volcano* which has been known to erupt, is at present not active but still shows signs that a future eruption is possible. The term comes from the French word, *dormir* – to sleep. Mt Vesuvius is dormant.

dormitory settlement: a small town or village where people who *commute* live. The settlement will be:

- quiet (from the French word *dormir* – to sleep) during the day when residents have commuted elsewhere to work
- accessible by road or rail to a larger settlement offering work opportunities
- suburbanised – having some of the features of the suburbs of the larger settlement e.g. evening entertainment facilities such as restaurants.

downward spiral: another name for a *vicious circle*. People or areas can become trapped in a spiral or cycle in which they either get poorer and poorer or simply cannot escape poverty. Periphery regions suffer downward spirals. (See *core and periphery, cycle of poverty* and *deprivation*).

drainage basin: the area of land drained by a river system. It is the system's water catchment area. The water in the *channels* of a river system does not

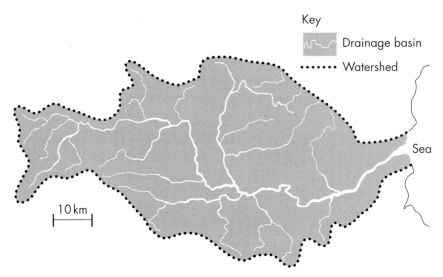

only come from rain falling directly into them, but also comes from the surrounding areas by surface *run-off* and *groundwater* flow. (See *watershed*.)

drought: a lack of rainfall over a long period of time. One of the worst droughts in recent times has been in the Sahel region of Africa where since 1968 rainfall has been very low. This has helped to cause *desertification* and famine in this region. In more recent years much of Britain and western Europe has been experiencing drought with consequent effects on natural environments and peoples' lifestyles.

drumlin: a large hummock of *boulder clay* deposited by an *ice sheet*. Drumlins:
● generally occur together as a group on lowland close to the mountainous areas from which the ice came e.g. north Lancashire close to the Lake District
● form low hills which resemble 'half-eggs' laid on their flat sides.

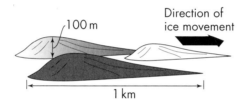

dry valley: a valley cut by running water which rarely contains water. During wet periods the water table may rise enough to give such a valley a temporary stream. They are common features of *chalk* and *limestone* areas, i.e. where there are *permeable* rocks which allow water to pass through them. Some geographers think that they were formed during the *Ice Age* when the ground was frozen and so not permeable. Meltwater from nearby ice could have run over this frozen, *impermeable* ground cutting out river-like valleys. (See *karst*).

dune: a mound or ridge of sand in a *desert* or on a *coastline* formed by the wind. In dry conditions wind transports sand, depositing some of it to form a dune. Some dunes are 'live' i.e. the wind blows the sand grains and so moves the dune. Two shapes of dune are found in deserts:
● barchans – are crescent-shaped
● seifs – are long, narrow ridges.
Belts of marine dunes can be found along stretches of the British coast e.g. between Southport and Blackpool westerly winds have transported and shaped sand into a belt of dunes behind the beach. Marine dune belts:

- provide protection for a coastline against the sea but
- may need stabilising by planting vegetation e.g. marram grass, to stop their migration inland.

dyke has three meanings in geography.
- A narrow ridge of igneous rock where molten *magma/lava* was injected vertically into the rocks underground. Since then the overlying rocks may have been eroded away leaving the dyke with its tough igneous rock as a ridge or wall e.g. Cleveland Dyke in north Yorkshire. It is an intrusive volcanic feature.
- A ditch or drainage channel in fenland areas e.g. Lincolnshire.
- An embankment built to prevent sea or river flooding e.g. Holland.

(See *intrusive vulcanicity*.)

dynamism: the idea that we live in an ever-changing world. Places change and we, as geographers:
- describe how they change and
- seek to explain why they changed.

Dynamism means change. Geographers study change over time at one particular place, and from place to place. For example, rainfall and the availability of water varies not only between London and Cyprus but also within London from year to year.

earthquake: a vibration or shaking movement of the Earth's crust. Major earthquakes occur at two types of *tectonic plate boundary*:
- *conservative boundaries* where plates can become locked together rather than sliding smoothly past each other
- *destructive boundaries* where one plate slips down below another causing friction and stresses as it does.

The intensity of earthquakes is measured on the *Richter Scale*. Earthquakes are a natural hazard for people and major ones often become disasters causing significant loss of life and destruction of property and facilities. *More economically developed countries* (MEDCs) and rural areas generally cope better than *less economically developed countries* (LEDCs) and urban areas in this respect. (See *epicentre* and *Pacific 'ring of fire'*.)

---

ecology is the study of the relationships between living things and their environment. Geographers are interested in:
- the way vegetation is linked with, for example, climate and soil
- how people and their environment interact – this has been called human ecology and is a key part of what geographers do.

---

economic development/growth: the process of creating more wealth for an area or country; it is perhaps the main way in which areas can change for the better. (See development, *less economically developed countries* (LEDCs) and *more economically developed countries* (MEDCs).

---

economies of scale: the cost savings that can be made when production is undertaken on a larger scale. Economies of scale can be:
- internal to a firm e.g. more labour employed which can then become specialised and more efficient, or new large machinery which can be kept running day and night so cutting costs
- external to a firm but available to a number in the area e.g. local banks developing special finance services or local colleges running special labour training courses or the sharing of transport facilities to reduce costs – external economies attract more firms into the area so encouraging *agglomeration*.

Bigger is often cheaper because of these economies of scale though firms may reach a size at which these cost savings stop – economies of scale have become diseconomies of scale.

ecosystem: the links which exist in an area between living things and their environmental surroundings. Within all areas climate, soil, slope and rock work together with plant and animal life to produce a particular total environment. A pond can be seen as an ecosystem with all the living and non-living parts being linked together and interacting one with another to form the pond system.

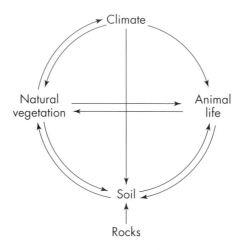

emergent coastline is a shoreline which is higher above sea level than it was in the past because:
- the land has risen or
- sea level has fallen.

This can happen as ice sheets either develop or melt on land areas. A raised beach is the best example of a feature produced by emergence of the land from the sea. *Raised beaches* and an emergent coastline can be found in west Scotland and around the Mediterranean.

emigration: international migration out of a country. Emigrants can be:
- voluntary migrants i.e. leaving for economic or family reasons e.g. Britons going to a better job in New Zealand and settling close to other family members
- forced migrants i.e. leaving for political or personal safety reasons e.g. Muslims escaping ethnic cleansing in Serbia.

(See *refugees*.)

employment structure: the proportion of the working population employed in each of the four sectors of industry – *primary, secondary, tertiary* and *quaternary*. The structure varies:

● within a country from region to region and town to town e.g. a fishing port such as Newlyn in a farming county like Cornwall will have a larger primary sector than a town such as Maidenhead in the London commuter belt with a growing number of hi-tech industries

● from country to country according to its stage of economic development. *more economically developed countries* (MEDCs) have large tertiary and quaternary sectors and *less economically developed countries* (LEDCs) large primary sectors.

Triangular graphs are commonly used to show differences in employment structure between countries, regions and towns.

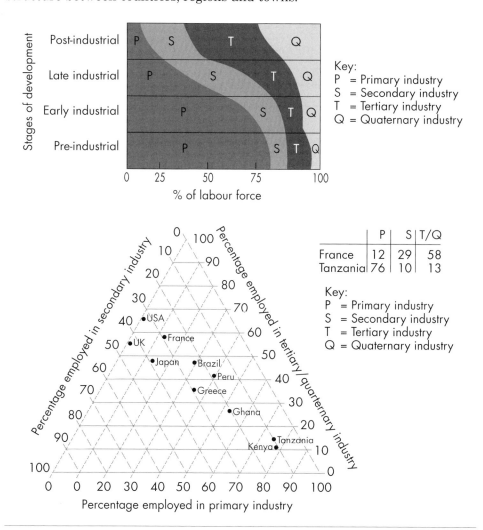

	P	S	T/Q
France	12	29	58
Tanzania	76	10	13

Key:
P = Primary industry
S = Secondary industry
T = Tertiary industry
Q = Quaternary industry

energy: the ability to do work. This ability is provided by supplies of fuel and power. Economic development requires these supplies, especially of electricity, to be available. Sources of these supplies are known as primary energy and are:
- *non-renewable* e.g. oil, coal
- *renewable* e.g. wind, waves, solar.

As the need for energy continues to grow worldwide and the non-renewable sources, upon which we still heavily rely, begin to run low in some parts of the world an energy supply crisis may face us in the future.

enterprise zone: a specific place identified by the British Government in which they offer financial incentives to industry. These zones are small localities where unemployment and the poor state of the environment is a problem. Firms which locate in enterprise zones are, for example, excused from paying business rates. (See *assisted areas* and *regional policy*.)

environmental hazards (See *hazards* and *natural hazards*.)

environmentally sensitive areas (ESAs) are areas in the UK of particular ecological and environmental importance. This means that:
- their natural landscape and ecosystems are to be conserved
- farmers are allowed to earn a reasonable income in them but must ensure that their farming methods fit in with this *conservation*.

environmental quality monitoring: the recording of opinions about the state of an environment, often an urban one, in which people live and/or work. Good quality environments are important to residents and workers in today's world. It is a reason why many people choose to live and/or work on the edge of urban areas, and to desert inner city areas if they have not been significantly improved. One popular way of monitoring environmental quality is for an observer to use an index such as the one for housing below.

epicentre: the point on the Earth's surface directly above where an *earthquake* starts deep in the Earth's crust. This starting point is known as the earthquake focus. The earthquake's tremors are likely to be about their strongest at the epicentre.

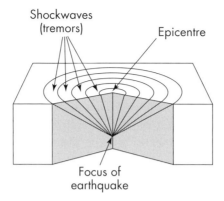

Shockwaves (tremors)

Epicentre

Focus of earthquake

equal opportunities: a policy adopted by many institutions to try to allow everyone, regardless of race, religion, gender or age, the chance to do their best. Equal opportunities policies are important in the study of:

- international migration
- the swing from manufacturing to service industries in *more economically developed countries* (MEDCs)
- regional development policy
- the redevelopment of inner city areas
- provision for the increasingly ageing populations of *more economically developed countries* (MEDCs).

equatorial climate: the hot, wet climate found on lowland areas up to about 10° latitude either side of the Equator. Temperatures are high all year round so the annual temperature range is small. Rainfall is high and occurs most afternoons as a result of convection following the midday heat. Rainforest is the natural vegetation type for this climate. Equatorial climates are found in Amazonia, Brazil and Indonesia. (See *convectional rain* and *tropical rainforest*.)

erosion: the wearing away of the Earth's surface by:

- running water
- moving ice
- the wind
- the sea.

Erosion includes *weathering* of rock and the transportation or removal of the weathered material. It is a key part of the continual and natural destruction-creation-destruction cycle of the Earth's surface. (See *deposition*.)

escarpment: a two-slope upland feature which forms much of the landscape of the *chalk* downs of southern England e.g. North and South Downs,

Chiltern Hills. Escarpments:
- have a short, steep scarp slope and a long, gentle dip slope
- have a dry, grassy surface
- have springs where the chalk meets an adjoining clay vale
- are often 200–300 metres above sea level.

estuary: the lower section of a river, close to its mouth, which is tidal thus allowing fresh water and sea water to mix. The rise in sea level at the end of the last *Ice Age* created many estuaries. Sea ports are often located in estuaries e.g. Tilbury on the Thames estuary.

ethnic area: one in which people of a particular racial and/or cultural group tend to congregate. This area is normally a distinct residential area of a town/city, and develops special ethnic and cultural characteristics which distinguish it from other areas. Most new incomers to a country seem to settle in the appropriate ethnic neighbourhood. Some of these are in the inner city and are deprived. Segregation according to ethnic origin occurs in urban areas in all countries. (See *deprivation*.)

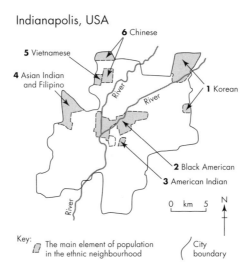

European Union (EU): the organisation which links 15 Western European countries. Cooperation and perhaps eventually integration of their economic, social and political life is the purpose of the EU. It has a number of institutions e.g. the Council of Ministers, the European Court of Justice, which pass policies and laws on certain subjects e.g. agriculture, employment rights etc. Removal of all trade barriers between member countries is one of the key features of the Union. Brussels has developed into its administrative capital. The 15 member countries include: France, Germany, Holland, Belgium, Italy, Luxembourg, U.K., Ireland, Denmark, Greece, Portugal, Spain, Sweden, Austria and Finland.

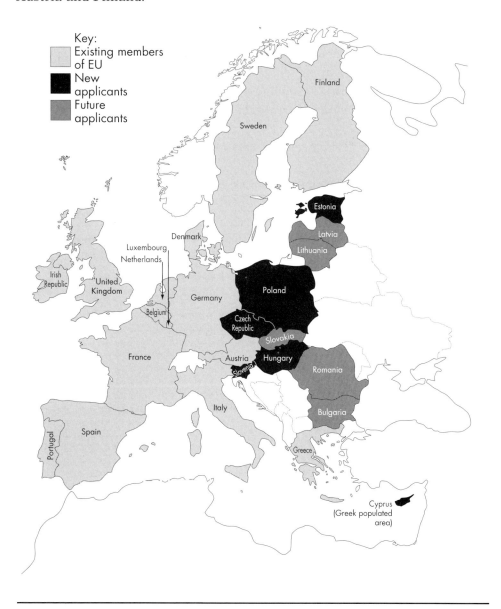

evapotranspiration: the loss of water into the atmosphere from the:

- ground
- water surfaces
- vegetation.

Evapotranspiration is a combined process of evaporation (i.e. loss from the ground and water surfaces) and transpiration (i.e. loss through the leaves of vegetation). It is an essential link in the *water (hydrological) cycle* and varies considerably according to:
- climatic factors such as temperature and wind speed
- the type and amount of vegetation.

exfoliation: takes place when boulders weather by layers peeling off one after another like an onion. This onion-peeling type of *mechanical weathering* occurs when stresses and pressures build up between the inside and outside of the rock because of:
- repeated temperature changes, say between hot days and cold nights as in a desert
- repeated wetting and drying of the rock, particularly in hot, wet climates such as Malaysia.

export: a good or service which leaves a country in a trading arrangement. Exports earn foreign currency for a country because people abroad pay for them and money enters the country. Exports can be:
- goods produced in the exporting country – known as visible exports e.g. cars
- goods bought from abroad but re-exported – known as visible entrepot exports. Singapore specialises in this type of trade
- services sold abroad – known as invisible exports e.g. foreign tourists.

extensive farming: farming activities spread over a large area of land on which little capital (e.g. equipment) and/or labour might be invested. Low yields per hectare are produced. The beef cattle ranches of the Argentine Pampas or the cereal farms of the North American Prairies are examples of extensive farming.

extractive industry: a type of *primary* industry which obtains raw materials from the ground e.g. coal mining, limestone quarrying, and the extraction of oil and metal ores such as copper, gold, etc. (See *primary products*.)

extrusive: the term for *magma/lava* that reaches the Earth's surface and solidifies to form landforms such as a volcanic cone or a lava flow. All eruptions of material directly on to the surface are called extrusive vulcanicity. (See *intrusive*.)

eye: the centre of a *hurricane* or tropical storm.

factors of production: the *resources* used to produce goods and services. There are four types of factor.

- Land, also known as natural resources – these are the free gifts of nature e.g. the ground, minerals.
- Labour, also known as human resources – this is people's mental and physical work.
- Capital and all the artificial aids used to make other goods e.g. machinery, money.
- Knowledge – the ideas, information and know-how about making things inherited or discovered by a generation e.g. the knowledge contained in books.

Production can use much more of one of these factors than the others so that it becomes for example *labour-intensive* e.g. teaching, or *capital-intensive* e.g. a robotic car factory.

factory farming: the rearing of animals, usually indoors, as a factory production line. Animals are:

- reared rapidly from birth to slaughter
- fed regularly, including with hormones
- kept in small spaces e.g. crates.

Chickens and pigs are the most commonly factory farmed animals. Factory farming has its opponents. It has helped to keep chicken, egg, pork and bacon prices lower.

famine: a serious shortage of food, causing people to die of starvation. The famines in some *Sahel* countries during the past 20 years have been put down to a combination of:

- climatic change, especially *drought*
- farmer's mismanagement of the land, especially overgrazing of pastures
- war dislocating farming and food distribution.

(See *desertification*.)

faulting is the:
- fracturing followed by
- displacement

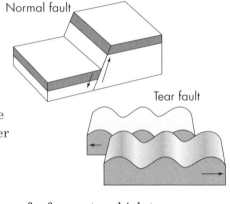

Normal fault

Tear fault

of rock by forces within the Earth's crust. Faults produced by faulting are natural vertical cracks between rocks which no longer match either side of the crack. This lack of match is because after fracturing the rocks:
- slip vertically or
- slide horizontally.

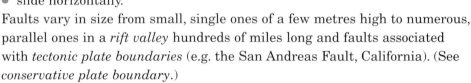

Faults vary in size from small, single ones of a few metres high to numerous, parallel ones in a *rift valley* hundreds of miles long and faults associated with *tectonic plate boundaries* (e.g. the San Andreas Fault, California). (See *conservative plate boundary*.)

feedback: the eventual effect of an event, for instance:
- a rising birth rate – will eventually lead to more parents which in time may again increase the birth rate
- a growing *core* region – may pull in resources from *periphery* regions but in time some of the benefits and resources of the core may flow back into periphery regions.

A farmer may plough back profits as inputs of capital investment in the farm, and this is also termed feedback. Feedback mechanisms set up new cycles and *systems*. They encourage change in the world. (See *cycle of decline or growth*.)

fertiliser is the material added by farmers to the soil in order to:
- replace nutrients taken out by growing plants
- improve crop yields and health.

Fertiliser can be:
- organic i.e. manure
- inorganic i.e. chemicals.

fertility has two meanings in geography.
- The average number of children each woman in a population, usually between 15 and 50 years of age, will bear. A fertility rate of two is likely to keep the total population stable.
- How suitable a soil is for the growth of plants and crops. A fertile soil allows them to grow quickly and well. The contents, texture and structure of the soil make it fertile or otherwise.

fjord: a U-shaped glacial trough found along a *coastline* which has been partly submerged by the sea. Such troughs are evidence of past:

- *glaciation*
- drowning.

They are:

- long, deep, narrow and steep-sided, and
- only found in once glaciated areas e.g. Norway and the south island of New Zealand.

Sogne Fiord, Norway is 177 km long, up to 4 km wide and up to 1,220 metres deep.

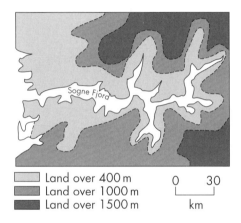

	Land over 400 m
	Land over 1000 m
	Land over 1500 m

0   30

km

flooding occurs when:

- water which is normally below ground (the *water table*) is in fact above it
- rivers carry more water (*discharge*) than they can contain within their banks.

A large but temporary increase in discharge is known as a flash flood. There are various causes of flooding:

- heavy rainfall
- melting snow
- greater surface *run-off* due to *deforestation* and urbanisation
- dam or embankment failure.

The number and intensity of floods can be reduced by:

- strengthening river banks
- deepening river *channels*
- building dams
- raising the level of a *flood plain*
- diverting rivers.

York has a long history of flooding by the river Ouse and a number of the above flood protection measures have been put in place.

flood plain: the flat land surrounding a river, usually in its lower course. The plain is formed of *alluvium* once transported by the river and later deposited when it flooded its low banks. (See *levee* and *meander*.)

flow line: a technique used on a map or diagram to show quantities of movement between two places, e.g. the percentage of passengers on various air routes from Heathrow.

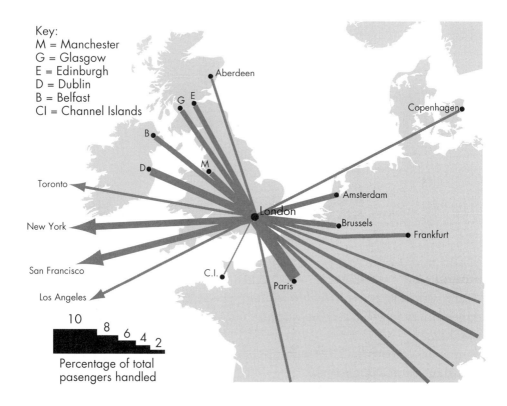

Key:
M = Manchester
G = Glasgow
E = Edinburgh
D = Dublin
B = Belfast
CI = Channel Islands

Aberdeen
Copenhagen
Toronto
New York
San Francisco
Los Angeles
C.I.
Paris
London
Amsterdam
Brussels
Frankfurt

10
8
6
4
2
Percentage of total pasengers handled

fluvial: a general term referring to the action of rivers. Fluvial processes include the types of *erosion* (e.g. *abrasion*, *hydraulic action*) and the types of transport and deposition (e.g. *suspension*, *solution*) undertaken by running water. They lead to the formation of fluvial landforms e.g. valleys, *waterfalls*. Meltwater around the edges of ice sheets and glaciers has a similar action in cold environments; this is referred to as fluvioglacial.

fodder crop is one grown specifically in order to feed livestock, especially those animals kept indoors during the winter. Dairy cattle farms in Britain often grow some oats and barley for this purpose.

fog: occurs when cloud at ground level reduces visibility to less than 1 km. It is caused by the cooling of moist air to its *dewpoint* temperature with the result that condensation of water vapour occurs. Cooling can take place:
- at night during a winter anticyclone when radiation of heat into space occurs
- when warm, moist air moves over a cold surface (known as advection fog)
- at a front.

Fog is most common on hills, in valleys or hollows, and over lakes, marshes and flood plains. Atmospheric pollution added to fog is known as smog. The Grand Banks off Newfoundland, with its advection fog, is generally the foggiest place in the world.

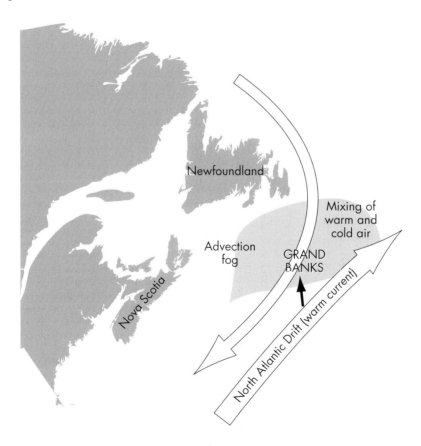

folding: the bending of a layer(s) of rock due to forces inside the Earth's crust. It can occur on various scales from small local folds of a few metres in size to continental fold mountains. Fold mountains occur at plate boundaries e.g. the Himalayas have been formed where the Indian and Eurasian Plates have collided.

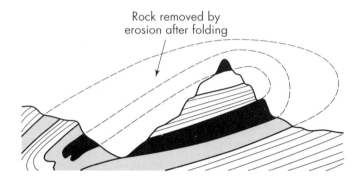

Rock removed by erosion after folding

food surplus: when the food supplied by farming exceeds that demanded by the public. So-called 'food mountains' have been a feature of the domestic economy in some *European Union* countries. The *Common Agricultural Policy* (CAP) system of guaranteed prices encouraged farmers to over-produce.

footloose: a type of industry which chooses a location tied to neither the location of its raw materials nor the location of a particular *market*. Such industries have a relatively free choice of location but are frequently attracted by high-quality transport facilities e.g. motorway junctions. Edge-of-town and *greenfield sites* often attract footloose industries e.g. *high-tech industries* and food processing companies. (See *material-orientation*.)

formal sector: that part of the economy which provides the country's official paid work. People may be working for either the state e.g. police, teachers or companies. Characteristics of work in the formal sector include:
- a contract covering hours and wages
- a set workplace e.g. a factory
- an income from which taxes are paid.

The formal sector can be split into *primary, secondary, tertiary* and *quaternary*. In *less economically developed countries* (LEDCs) it is estimated that only about 40% of the working population are employed in this sector. This is clearly a larger sector in *more economically developed countries* (MEDCs). (See *employment structure* and *informal sector*.)

fossil fuels: the remains of past vegetation which are now used as a source of *energy* e.g. coal, oil and natural gas. These fuels took enormous periods of time to form and so are described as *non-renewable*. The bulk of the world's energy is produced from them, and their burning to produce heat energy is a major source of atmospheric pollution. Over-reliance on a polluting and non-renewable energy source is one of the world's main geographical issues.

fragile environment is usually a natural environment which is particularly sensitive to the actions of people. It can easily be harmed by direct or indirect human action. Once damaged, repair is likely to be slow or even impossible. The Earth's environments are all fragile but some more so than others. Environmental damage in the most fragile and delicate areas is clearly visible:
- tropical coral reefs such as Australia's Great Barrier Reef
- the Alaskan tundra
- tourist *honeypots* in British National Parks.
Protection to save many fragile environments may be necessary.

freeze–thaw: the *weathering* process which shatters rocks during frosty spells. When water in cracks, joints or spaces in rock freezes. Its volume expands and pressure is exerted on the surrounding rock. Repeated freezing and pressure will shatter the rock. Frost shattering of rock in this way is a type of *mechanical weathering*, and leads to the development of *scree* slopes.

friction of distance: See *distance-decay*.

front: an *air mass* boundary. It divides air of different properties e.g. warm from cold. A *depression* contains either two fronts:
- a *warm front* and
- a *cold front*
or an occluded front where the two have joined. Fronts are associated with cloud, rain and the uplift of air. (See *occlusion*.)

functions are the main activities, services and jobs provided in a settlement for its population and visitors. They can be divided into:
- *low-order* functions – frequently used everyday needs e.g. a post office, a newsagent which need only a small threshold population to survive
- *middle-order* functions – regularly but not daily used services e.g. a bank, a library
- *high-order* functions – occasionally used services e.g. a concert hall, an art gallery.

The larger the settlement the more and the higher the order of functions to be found. Cities provide numerous functions of all three orders; villages are likely to provide only a few low-order functions. (See *threshold population*.)

functional zone: an area of a settlement in which a certain type of land use (e.g. shops and offices) and/or social group of people (e.g. middle income home-owners) are concentrated. Such concentrations exist in towns and cities to produce a pattern of functional zones as shown below.

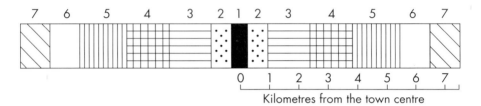

Kilometres from the town centre

3 Zone of industry and Victorian houses
5 Suburban housing built since 1945
1 Central business district
6 Green belt
2 Zone of urban renewal
7 Zone of commuter villages
4 Zone of housing, including council estates built before 1939

gabions are wire baskets filled with rock and placed at the foot of an eroding cliff. They are generally used along with other measures to try to slow down wave *erosion* of a *coastline*. At Overstrand along the north Norfolk coast they are placed at the foot of a sea wall. They are a relatively cheap coastal protection method.

general circulation: the broad pattern of the world's major winds. This circulation:
- seeks to transfer heat from the Equator towards the Poles
- blows over the Earth's surface from areas of permanent high pressure (e.g. the Tropics) to areas of permanent low pressure (e.g. the Arctic/Antarctic Circles)
- blows in the upper atmosphere in the opposite way to its surface/surface directory.

The westerly winds which blow over the surface of Britain for much of the year are part of the general circulation.

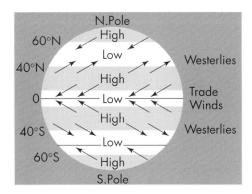

gentrification: the improving of a low-income area in a town/city when older properties are bought and done up by people on a higher income. These higher-income people might be young working couples without children. The *accessibility* of old inner city areas for work and entertainment might encourage gentrification. Islington in north London began its gentrification in the 1970s.

geomorphic processes are the types of *erosion* and *deposition* which help to produce *landforms*. Geomorphology is the study of landform formation. Landforms are the result of:
- geomorphic processes acting upon
- the rocks of the Earth's surface.

Abrasion by the waves or the deposition of silt by a river are geomorphic processes.

geothermal energy: the heat and electricity obtained from hot water from the Earth's interior. As a source of energy it is:
- clean
- renewable
- relatively cheap.

Iceland and New Zealand are important producers.

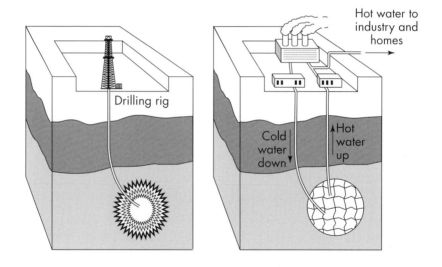

ghetto: an area of a city dominated by an ethnic or minority group of people. Urban ghettos are inferior to other areas of the city in terms of:
- the quality of the housing (e.g. overcrowded rooms)
- the number and range of amenities (e.g. few shops and little entertainment)
- the level of crime and violence (e.g. high drug and gang activity).

Many big American cities have ghettos where people live in rundown, squalid conditions and are trapped in a cycle of poverty (deprivation).

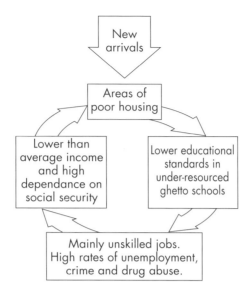

glacial trough: another name for a U-shaped valley. They are valleys found in once- or presently-*glaciated* uplands which are:

- wide
- flat-floored
- steep-sided.

The movement of a glacier down a previously more V-shaped river valley has deepened and widened it. Some glacial troughs now have ribbon lakes in them e.g. Lake Ullswater in the English Lake District. (See *hanging valley*.)

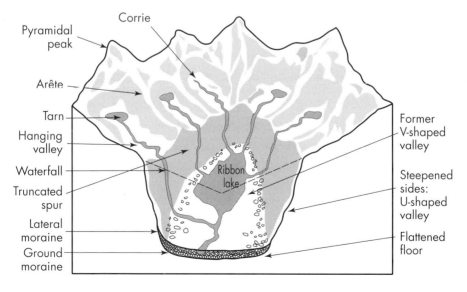

glaciation: a long period of low temperatures, heavy snow and advancing ice. Glaciers move down valleys in uplands and can join to form ice sheets covering lowlands. The ice and its meltwater shape the landscape during *glaciation*. Greenland and Antarctica are being glaciated today. Britain was glaciated several times during the past three million years; a period known as the *Ice Age*.

glacier: a body of ice which flows down a valley.. It starts from a corrie and alters the shape of the valley to a U-shaped trough as it flows down.
See *corrie, glacial trough, ice sheet and moraine*.

gley: a saturated soil. It develops in poorly drained conditions, often on level ground at the foot of a slope. It is a blue/greyish coloured soil but there may be orange streaks deep in the soil. In summer the *water table* in the soil may drop and any iron at this level will oxidise to form these streaks. See *Saturation*.

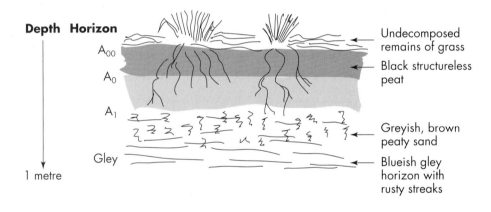

globalisation: the idea that an increasing number of geographical systems are worldwide ones. We live in a world in which people, places, production and the environment are becoming ever more interdependent. For example, a physical event such as a major volcanic eruption or an economic event such as an industrial dispute in Korea, can have serious effects in other parts of the globe.

global shift: the industrialisation of *newly industrialising countries* (NICs), at about the same time as the de-industrialisation of the older industrialised countries. NICs are found around the western rim of the Pacific in particular (e.g. Taiwan, Korea); older industrialised countries include those in Western Europe. Manufacturing industry has been shifting location and ownership during the second half of the 20th century. Asian car manufacturers now produce more than European and American manufacturers. Many of these manufacturers are *multinational or transnational companies* (MNCs or TNCs) e.g. Nissan.

global warming: the rise in average world temperatures during the second half of the 20th century. There are two possible explanations.
The cause is artificial. People have been increasing the amount of certain gases, especially carbon dioxide in the atmosphere through various activities e.g. industrial pollution, car exhausts. These gases may increase the natural *greenhouse effect* in the atmosphere which traps heat close to the Earth.
The cause is natural. Climate change e.g. the *Ice Age* has occurred throughout history i.e. long before people began polluting the atmosphere. The Sun, for instance, seems to have radiated more and less heat at different times in the past.
Melting glaciers and ice caps in various parts of the world are an effect of global warming. It is not known how different areas will be affected if global warming continues. The cause and time-span of the warming may become clearer in time. Governments for instance at the 1998 Kyoto Conference however, are beginning to agree that we should reduce the emission of polluting gases in case they are causing global warming by strengthening the greenhouse effect.

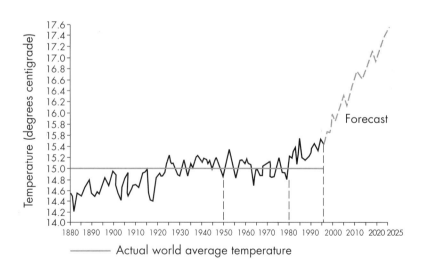

— Actual world average temperature

gorge: a narrow, steep-sided valley cut through hard rock such as *carboniferous limestone*. Winnats Pass, Castleton, Derbyshire is a limestone gorge which is thought to have been formed when the roof of an underground cavern collapsed. Canyons are a type of gorge.

government subsidy: money paid by a government, including the
European Union institutions, to a group or organisation within that country.
It might be thought to be in the interests of the general public that money be
granted to, for example:
- industries in a region with high unemployment in order to keep them in
  business and so protect jobs
- theatres in order to keep down the price of tickets and so help them to
  stay open.

Government subsidies are an important part of the government's regional
development policy in many countries. (See *common agricultural policy* and
regional policy.)

gradient: the slope of the land between any two points. It can be measured
as follows, usually from an Ordnance Survey map:

$$\text{Gradient} = \frac{\text{Vertical rise (difference between the contours in metres)}}{\text{Horizontal Distance (distance over the ground in metres/km)}}$$

Gradients are stated as either:
- a ratio e.g. 1 in 10, which means that for every 10 metres over the ground
  the slope goes up or down 1 metre.
- a percentage e.g. 10%, which is 1 in 10.

graphicacy: the drawing of maps and diagrams in order to communicate
geographical information. Cartographers are map makers. The 'graphy' in
geography refers to this distinctive way of communicating information, which
geographers use extensively.

green belt: an area surrounding a large town/city which should not be built
upon. It should:
- be preserved as open space and used only for farming and recreation
- halt the spread of the urban area into the countryside.

The first green belt was introduced around London in 1947. Some local
planning authorities have ignored the green belt and allowed building on
the edge of the town/city, especially when the demand for local housing is
great. green belts are not always belt-shaped. There are green wedges, green
hearts, green fingers and green buffers. (See *urban sprawl*).

green revolution: an agricultural revolution in some *less economically
developed countries* (LEDCs). Since the 1960s new varieties of grain crop e.g.
wheat and rice have been introduced into agriculture in these countries. The
varieties grow very fast, producing high *yields* and more than one harvest

per year. India has become largely self-sufficient in food because of the use of such crops, alongside:

- chemical fertilisers, insecticides and fungicides
- *irrigation*
- *mechanisation.*

greenfield site: land that has previously not been used for industrial or urban development. It is likely to be in the countryside or on the edge of an urban area. Many companies building houses, owning supermarkets or making manufactured goods favour locations on green, open land; the quality of the environment for living and/or working can be higher in such locations. (See *brownfield site high-tech industry and urban sprawl.*)

greenhouse effect: the process in the lower atmosphere by which heat radiated from the Earth's surface is prevented from escaping into space by the presence of certain 'gases' and cloud. Carbon dioxide is the main 'greenhouse gas' responsible for re-radiating back down to the Earth's surface. Pollution of the atmosphere by human activities has increased the amount of greenhouse gas in the atmosphere. The natural greenhouse effect may therefore have been strengthened causing *global warming.*

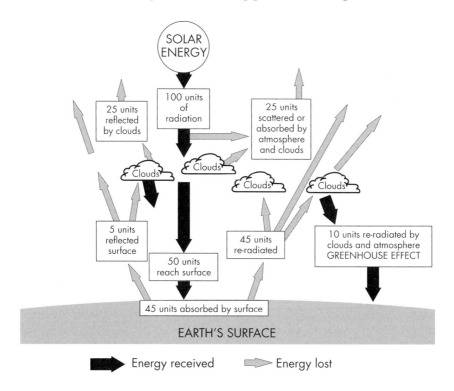

grid reference: a pair of coordinates on an Ordnance Survey map which allows places to be identified. four-figure references identify a grid square with six-figure references being used to pinpoint particular places within the square. The sequence for stating a six-figure reference is:

- start in the bottom left corner of the map
- work horizontally along the bottom of the map giving the two-figure number at the left edge of the square in which the place is this is called an easting
- estimate how many tenths of the way across this square the place is
- work vertically up the left side of the map giving first, the two-figure number at the bottom edge of the square, and then estimate the number of tenths counting upwards. It is the same method as along the easting edge of the map this edge is called the northing.

Eastings are always given before northings.

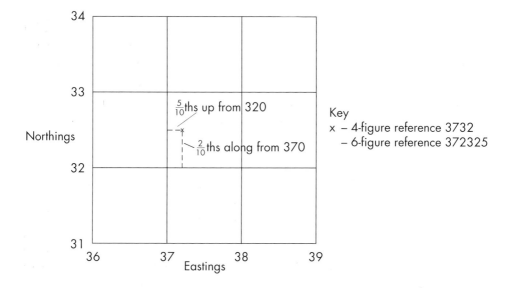

gross domestic/national product per person (GDP and GNP per person) are two commonly used measures of a country's level of economic development. They are measured similarly but include slightly different items.

$$\text{GDP per person} = \frac{\text{total value of all goods and services produced in a country in a year}}{\text{total population of the country}}$$

It does not include income from abroad but does include the production of foreign-owned firms within the country. The Nissan and Samsung factories, for example, in Britain do contribute to raising our GDP.

$$\text{GDP per person} = \frac{\text{total value of all goods and services produced by firms owned by citizens of that country}}{\text{total population of the country}}$$

This time income from investments abroad is included but production by foreign-owned firms within the country is not. Nissan and Samsung do not raise Britain's GNP.

In the case of Britain:

- the 'domestic' in GDP means production on British territory
- the 'national' in GNP means production from British ownership.

They are usually expressed in US dollars.(See *economic development, human welfare and quality of life*.)

ground water: the water stored in *permeable* rocks underground. It collects as water infiltrates down through soil and rock. Gravity causes groundwater to flow. (See *aquifer, hydrological cycle, infiltration and water table*.)

growing season: that part of the year during which average daily temperatures are above 6°C. Most crops will not grow until this temperature is reached. In Britain the number of growing season months varies from over eight in Cornwall to less than five in northern Scotland. Few crops survive frost so the number of days in a year when frost is very unlikely to occur will be important in calculating the length of the growing season. On the Canadian Prairies, spring-sown wheat requires a frost-free period of at least 100 days.

growth pole: the place within an area where economic growth is concentrated. It will be an economic core with new investment, industrial development and growing wealth. Growth poles are:

usually parts or all of a town/city e.g. the London Docklands.

often able to stimulate regional development. (the surrounding region may begin to develop as the effects of growth at the pole spill over into it(the British government hopes that this will happen after they have helped to set up a small *enterprise zone* in an *assisted area*. (See *core and periphery*.)

groyne: a barrier, usually wooden, built at an angle to a beach in order to reduce *longshore drift*. They can successfully prevent the loss of sand and shingle from a tourist beach but can deny another beach along the coast of a supply of these materials. They are a very popular method of coastal protection and used by many resorts along the south coast of England e.g. at Bournemouth.

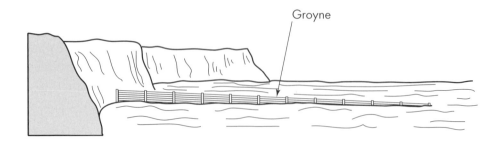

Groyne

guest worker: an economic migrant. Such people will have migrated from one country to another in search of work, and may stay only a short period of time. Guest workers, known as gastarbeiter, have been attracted, especially from southern and eastern Europe (e.g. Turkey), to jobs in Germany. They often provide cheap labour and fill jobs unpopular with the local population e.g. waiters. (See *migration*.)

gulf stream: a warm *ocean current* that flows north from the Gulf of Mexico. The part that crosses the North Atlantic is known as the North Atlantic Drift and helps to keep Britain and north-west Europe warmer than it otherwise would be, especially in winter.

gully: a narrow *channel*, more than half a metre deep, on a slope, often a hillside. It is formed by running water, usually by rapid *run-off* after heavy rain. Gullying is a major type of soil erosion and is a particular problem where:
- there is no vegetation to bind the soil together
- farmers continue to plough land up and down the slope so forming furrows which heavy rainfall can enlargen to form gullies.

The Badlands of South Dakota, USA are the most famous example of a gullied area. *Afforestation* of slopes helps to prevent gullying. The slopes around British reservoirs are usually planted with trees. (See *Contour Ploughing* and *Soil Erosion*.)

H

habitat: the natural home of a plant, animal or living community. Specific environmental conditions will be suitable for its growth and survival. Modern intensive agriculture in *more economically developed countries* (MEDCs) has destroyed several wildlife habitats e.g. hedgerows.

hamlet: a small rural settlement that is bigger than an isolated dwelling but smaller than a village. A population of 11,100 and the odd *low-order* service e.g. a public house is typical of a hamlet. Kirby Grindalythe on the Yorkshire Wolds with its 12 houses and a church is an example.

hanging valley: a valley which joins a U-shaped *glacial trough* at a level higher than the trough floor. The valley 'hangs' above the main U-shaped valley and any stream or river in it will enter the main valley as a waterfall. The cause of the 'hanging' is the greater deepening of the main U-shaped valley during *glaciation*.

hazard: something that threatens human life and property. There are two kinds.
- A natural hazard e.g. an earthquake threat. Earthquakes occur occasionally but can kill large numbers of people and are the result of the forces of nature.
- A human or artificial hazard e.g. the threat of a road traffic accident. These may occur more frequently but likely to kill fewer people.

A hazard becomes a disaster when a threatened event actually happens destroying human lives and property.

headland: a stretch of high *coastline* made of solid rock and projecting out into the sea. It will be formed of harder rock than the surrounding coastline. Wave *erosion* is likely to be active along the coastline. Headlands are also known as capes. Flamborough Head on the Yorkshire coast is an example. (See *cliffs, caves, and stacks*.)

heat island a large urban area that is warmer than the surrounding countryside. The heat island effect is generally stronger at night and during

winter. There are various causes:

- artificial heating from homes, offices, factories and cars
- lower wind speeds in urban areas with consequent reduction of heat loss
- good drainage in urban streets with consequent reduction of evaporation and thus heat loss
- greater absorption of natural heat by urban buildings.

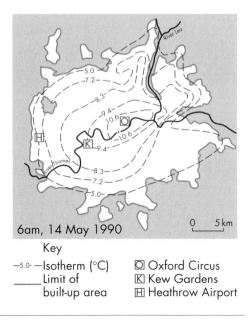

6am, 14 May 1990

Key

−5.0− Isotherm (°C)

⎯⎯ Limit of built-up area

◙ Oxford Circus

Ⓚ Kew Gardens

⊞ Heathrow Airport

heavy industry: manufacturing industry which:

- uses large amounts of heavy raw materials
- produces bulky finished products.

The steel industry is an example. Heavy industry often chooses material-orientated locations. It is a declining type of manufacturing in most *more economically developed countries* (MEDCs) at present.

hierarchy: the ranking of geographical features such as settlements, services and rivers in order of size and importance. The settlement hierarchy of a region might range from cities to hamlets and will be linked to a service hierarchy e.g. many and *high-order* services in the few cities, and few and *low-order* services in the many hamlets.

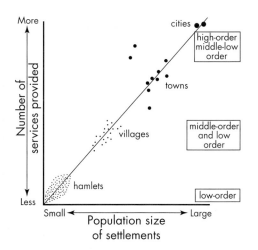

high-order a type of: service or function provided in certain settlements e.g. a concert hall or department store. These are used more infrequently by people and need a large population before they are provided.

High-order can also describe a shopping centre within a large settlement e.g. the *central business district* (CBD) Here, high-order means the most important shopping area. This will be where the choice of goods and services is greatest, and where high-order services or functions are available. (See *threshold population*.)

high-tech industry: modern industry which uses a lot of capital, knowledge and advanced technology. The production of computer, micro-electronic and telecommunication equipment is an example High-tech industries:

● produce small components and products made of plastic, rubber and glass
● need highly skilled workers and new ideas
● need to be accessible to air and quick road transport facilities for moving their products.
● favour *greenfield sites* close to universities.

The M4 corridor is the location of many high-tech industries. (See *accessibility, science park*.)

high-yielding variety (HYV): a special variety of a crop that has been bred scientifically to produce bigger yields than the crop normally does. Special varieties of wheat and rice have been a key part of the green revolution. IR8 rice improved rice yields in the Philippines by 500 % during the 1960s.

hill farming: largely involves sheep rearing on uplands and moorlands. Sheep are often the only type of farming possible in these environments where winters are hard and soils thin. Such farming is *extensive*. On the open fells (hills) of the Lake District sheep are grazed while crops (e.g. oats, vegetables, grass) can be grown on the better agricultural land in the valley bottoms. These crops are often grown as animal fodder. (See *fodder crops*.)

hinterland: a *sphere of influence*, usually that of a port. It is the area around the port with which it trades in other words:

● the source of its supplies for export
● the destination of its imports.

Large ports such as Rotterdam have hinterlands covering the whole country i.e. Holland as well as parts of other countries e.g. Belgium, Germany. The term hinterland is sometimes used to refer to the sphere of influence of a large inland city. (See *urban field*.)

homeworking: earning income from work done at home. For example:
- professional knowledge-based work, perhaps using computers, faxes and e-mail; teleputing involves working at home and communicating with head office via computer technology.
- low-paid, labour-intensive work. Some sewing and packing has long been done for companies in homes.

honeypot: a site which attracts large numbers of tourists. Tourism can threaten attractive natural landscape of the countryside honeypots because of the:
- traffic congestion
- crowding leading to litter, noise and soil damage.

The Major Oak in Sherwood Forest is a tourist honeypot.

horizon: a distinct layer within a *soil profile*. Normally soils can be divided into up to four horizons.
- The H-horizon – *humus* and decaying vegetation
- The A-horizon – the upper layer of organic matter and minerals
- The B-horizon – the sub-soil containing more inorganic material, especially minerals washed down from A.
- The C-horizon – weathered rock fragments just above the parent material e.g. bedrock.

horticulture: the growing of flowers, fruit and vegetables. It is highly *intensive* farming and carried out:
- in the open, especially when and where temperatures are higher e.g. the Californian summer
- under shelter e.g. glasshouses outside the warmest season.

hostile environment: a region of the world in which natural conditions, particularly climate are generally unwelcoming to human life. There are five such regions:
- The polar ice *deserts* of Antarctica and around the North Pole.
- The tundra (i.e. edge of the ice caps) and taiga (i.e. coniferous pine forests) regions of Scandinavia and northern Canada and Russia.
- The hot deserts of Africa, Australia and the Middle East.
- The hot, wet equatorial forests of Brazil, Central Africa and the East Indies.
- The high mountains and deserts deep in the middle of continents.

They are either sparsely populated or uninhabited. (See *Density of Population*.)

human welfare: the well-being of people. Industry and *economic development* create wealth. Greater wealth can benefit the general well-being of people – they can become safer, securer and/or happier. Ordinary people's needs are being met because wealth is being spent on items such as health and education which improve the quality of people's lives. *Quality of life* indexes which include such indicators as:
- the *infant mortality rate*
- *life expectancy*
- the *literacy rate*

are used to give a picture of the level of human welfare in an area.

humidity: the amount of water vapour there is in the air. It can be measured as follows.
- Absolute humidity – the total amount of water vapour in a certain volume of air.
- Relative humidity – the amount of water vapour present in the air as a percentage of the maximum it could hold at that temperature when saturated. The air is saturated at 100% relative humidity. The *dew point* has been reached and *condensation* will occur.

Relative humidity is measured by a *hygrometer*.

humus is a soil component. It is made up of decomposed organic matter and forms the top *horizon* in most soil profiles. It is dark brown in colour and is an important source of minerals for soil fertility.

hurricane: a violent, revolving tropical storm. Hurricanes are *cyclones* or low pressure areas which bring:
- winds of up to force 12 on the *Beaufort Scale*
- dense, dark thunderstorm clouds and very heavy rainfall

to the Gulf of Mexico region, especially in late summer. They are a natural *hazard* and often bring disaster.

hydraulic action: the mechanical loosening and sweeping away of materials by the power of moving water in a river or the sea. For example:
- in a river the water picks up loose fragments where it comes in to contact with the bank, and forms a plunge pool where water tumbles over a waterfall on to rock below
- along a coastline waves lash the cliff face forcing air into tiny cracks. The pressure enlargens the crack and weakens the cliff. It is a form of *erosion*.

hydro-electric power (HEP): electricity generated by moving water. It is a *renewable* source of energy. HEP stations are usually located in mountainous areas where rainfall, lakes and steep slopes are plentiful e.g. Scotland, Switzerland.

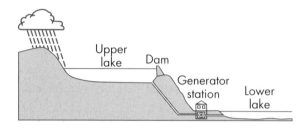

hydrograph: a diagram drawn to show changes in the rate of *discharge* of a river over a period of time. It is usual to also show rainfall on a *hydrograph* so that the link between discharge and rainfall can be examined.

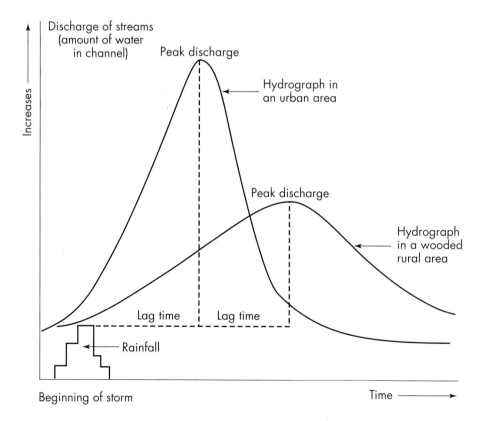

hydrological cycle: the *water cycle*. Water moves through this cycle as either a liquid or a vapour. A number of processes, such as *condensation,* and a number of stores, such as *groundwater* are involved in this transfer system. (See *precipitation*, *evapotranspiration*, *run-off*, infiltration and *throughflow*.)

hydrolysis: a form of *chemical weathering*. Certain minerals are altered chemically when they react with water. For example, felspar is a mineral found in granite. It reacts with water to form kaolin, a white clay called china clay. Hydrolysis leads in this way to the weathering of granite.

hygrometer: an instrument for measuring the relative *humidity* of the air. It consists of two thermometer bulbs: a wet and a dry.

hypermarket: a very large supermarket, perhaps containing other retailers under its roof. They sell a wide range of goods, including *high-order* ones e.g. jewellery, dishwashers and some consumer services e.g. banking, travel agency. They are usually found in out-of-town locations, perhaps on the *urban-rural fringe* where there is:
- easy access for car drivers
- ample space for building large car parks.

hypothesis: a testable statement. Testing hypotheses by means of fieldwork is popular in geography. By collecting factual information, hypotheses such as:
- rivers flow faster nearer their mouths
- land values decrease away from the *central business district* (CBD)
can be proved or disproved.

ice age: a period when ice has spread to cover areas not normally covered. The most recent of these periods occurred between about three million years and 10,000 years ago. It is generally known as the Ice Age. During it:
- the ice cap over the Arctic and North Pole spread southwards
- glaciers developed in and flowed from the Lake District, the Welsh Mountains and the Scottish Highlands
- these glaciers, at times, covered Britain with ice sheets as far south as a line between Bristol and the Thames
- the ice, at times, retreated northwards to again later advance southwards.

The cause of these very cold periods is not certain but the effects are clearly visible for very long periods afterwards. (See *glaciation*.)

ice sheet: a great mass of ice covering a large area of land. An ice sheet which is up to 3 km thick covers the landscape of Greenland today. During the *Ice Age* one ice sheet covered Scandinavia, the North Sea and much of Britain. (See *glaciation*.)

igneous: the name of a major group of rocks. They are those which are formed by the cooling and solidification of molten rock (*magma*) from beneath the Earth's crust. They are normally crystalline. *Lava* forms igneous rock. Granite and basalt are examples. (See *extrusive* and *intrusive*.)

immigration: the *migration* of people into a country from another. Those settling in the receiving country are known as immigrants. International migration can be:
- voluntary, perhaps for financial reasons and those peoples involved are known as economic immigrants
- forced because of persecution and genuine hardship; refugees and political immigrants fall into this group. (See *emigration* and *push-and-pull model*.)

impermeable: a characteristic of rock. It describes those rocks which do not allow water to pass through them because they are either:
- non-*porous* i.e. contain no pore-spaces to absorb water, or
- impervious i.e. contain no joints or cracks through which water can pass.

Clay is impermeable though porous. Impermeable rock surfaces lead to more *run-off* and give rise to more streams and rivers. (See *permeable*.)

import: a purchase by residents of a country from another country of:
- goods – known as visible imports e.g. Sri Lankan tea drunk in Britain
- services – known as invisible imports e.g. British holiday-makers in Spain.

Exports can pay for some or all import purchases. When export income does not cover most of a country's import bill, it may decide to try to control imports by, for example, putting a tax on some imported goods. More economically developed countries often import many *primary products* whereas manufactured goods may be important imports in less economically developed countries.

industrial estate: a specially selected area for industry in a town/city. Such estates are usually:
- purpose-built with a planned layout
- away from residential areas and the town's CBD (*Central business district*).
- good road network within them and near an existing outside network e.g. ring road junctions
- new factory units equipped with electricity, water, etc.
- made up of *footloose*, light industries
- more common in the older industrial areas of Britain where the need for employment has been greatest. (See *business / science / technology park*, *brownfield site*, *greenfield site* and *enterprise zone*.)

industrial inertia: the tendency for an industry to remain at a location even though the initial reasons for that choice are no longer as important. There may now be better locations for the industry e.g. at a motorway junction but it stays put, perhaps for personal reasons or the high cost involved in re-locating. Some of Sheffield's remaining steelworks may be geographically inert; local supplies of raw materials ran out some time ago.

industrial revolution is an enormous change in either:
- the amount of *industry* i.e. industrialisation occurs in a country e.g. the Old Industrial Revolution in Britain between around 1760 and 1840 or the process that has been happening in the *newly industrialising countries* (NICs) of South-East Asia since the 1960s or
- the type of industry i.e. industry changes to new products and ways of production. The New Industrial Revolution in the *more economically developed countries* (MEDCs) over the past 30 years has been based on the use of computer-based high-tech.

Modern industry in Britain differs from older industries in a number of ways. It is:

- *high-tech* and more automatised
- *footloose*
- light
- varied and flexible.

Its development has followed earlier *de-industrialisation*.

infant mortality rate: the number of deaths among under-one year olds in a year for every live birth in that year. It measures how many infants survive their first year of life as a key indicator of a country's level of development and the way in which it provides sanitation, nutrition and medical care for its people.

In 1996 it was:

- 9 in Britain (though 500 in 1850)
- 43 in Mexico
- 102 in Tanzania

(See *development, life expectancy* and *quality of life.*)

infiltration is the downward movement of water from the surface into the soil. The rate of infiltration depends upon:

- the amount and intensity of rainfall
- the amount of surface water
- the amount of water already in the soil
- the vegetation cover
- the *permeability* and compactness of the soil.

Once in the soil, water may pass into the bedrock (i.e. percolation) to form the groundwater. (See *hydrological cycle.*)

informal sector: that part of a country's employment which is paid but casual. The work is often:

- self-employed
- irregular
- part-time
- illegal e.g. without paying taxes; prostitution; while receiving state benefits.

Informal employment is common in *less economically developed countries'* (LEDCs) cities, often accounting for about half of the workers especially in:

- service employment e.g. shoe cleaning, street trading, carting
- small craft industries e.g. wood carving

In *more economically developed countries* (MEDGs) there is a significant amount of this sort of employment e.g. working in the evening for cash-only in addition to a normal day job. It is known as the black economy. (See *formal sector.*)

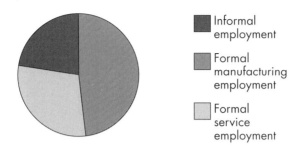

Informal employment

Formal manufacturing employment

Formal service employment

infrastructure: the basic framework of facilities that service an industrial country e.g. roads, railways, telephones, power and water supplies, education and training facilities, hospitals, etc. Developing an efficient infrastructure for industry and the community is a long and expensive process but essential if economic development is to occur. Building this infrastructure is a problem for many *less economically developed countries* (LEDCs) and keeping it updated is something *more economically developed countries* MEDCs need to keep their eye on (e.g. the transport infrastructure in London and to and from the Channel Tunnel).

in-migration: the movement of people into a new area from elsewhere in the same country. This could take the form of:
- people settling in a city from another city or from the countryside
- people settling in the countryside from a city.

(See *migration.*)

inner city: the area of older residential and industrial development lying between the centre and suburbs of a city. In many cities this is where physical, social and economic problems – usually called *urban deprivation* – are concentrated. There has often been a rapid run-down of employment and population in the area. Their need for special attention because of the scale and intensity of these problems is often great. Gradually, they are being redeveloped by either:
- the local authority or government e.g. the London Docklands or
- wealthier people and families i.e. being *gentrified* (e.g. Islington, north London).

(See *urban structure, urban decay* and *urban regeneration.*)

input is any item or *factor of production* (e.g. capital, raw materials etc.) put into a *system*. Inputs lead to outputs (i.e. production) from the system. Inputs into a farm system are seeds, fertilisers, the weather, etc.

insolation is the amount of heat energy radiated by the Sun which the Earth receives. It varies according to:
- latitude – being greatest at the Equator and least at the Poles
- season – more during the longer days of summer than in winter
- atmospheric condition – cloud and pollution cut down the amount of insolation.

See *general circulation* and *greenhouse effect*.

instability: a condition of the atmosphere in which air continues to rise. Instability of air means that cloud and possibly rain will occur. Continued rising and cooling can be to height condensation will take place. (See *stability*, *condensation* and *cloud*.)

integration is the process of linking up or joining together items to form a whole or a system. Geography is an integrating subject; it looks at the links between the various aspects of the environment. Integration is particularly important in the following areas.
- In Britain this older development dates mainly from the 19th century.
- Industry – many large factories e.g. car and steelworks are integrated with all the processes carried out under one roof. Two or more companies can integrate by bringing together all their activities.
- Transport – many cities now use an integrated transport scheme to try to manage traffic better. In these schemes different forms of transport are linked together e.g. car parks at edge-of-town tram stops.
- Politics – regions and countries can join together e.g. the *European Union* is an integrated group of countries with many common government policies.

intake: part of the land on a hill farm. It is the grazing land taken in from the hilly ground, or fell in the Lake District, and enclosed by walling. Rough grazing may also occur on the open fell above. Below the intake land will be the more level and productive inbye land on a Lake District *hill farm*.

intensive is the term used to describe any farming system which uses a high proportion of labour, capital or knowledge in relation to land. This generally means a high output per hectare of land. Farming in most parts of Britain is intensive. Market gardening is one of the most intensive types of farming;

high yields of vegetables, saladstuff
and flowers are achieved from
small areas of land because large
quantities of fertilisers, technology,
labour, etc. are used. The general
intensification of farming has been
a feature of more economically
developed countries *more economi-*
cally developed countries (MEDCs)

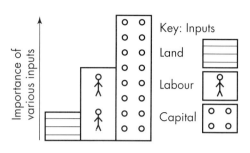

during this century. Farmland has been used more intensively as farming
has become increasingly mechanised, scientific and business-like. (See
agribusiness and *factors of production*.)

interception: the process by which rain is prevented from falling directly
onto the ground by trees and plants. It helps to slow down *run-off* and makes
flooding less likely. (See *hydrological cycle*.)

interdependence: the linking of places, industries and countries through
trade, aid and investment. The whole globe is now interdependent, with countries and their industries being dependent on other countries and industries
in other countries e.g. *more economically developed countries* (MEDCs) export
manufactured goods to l*ess economically developed countries* (LEDCs) made
from raw materials previously imported from them. *Multi-national companies*
link countries and their industries. (See *globalisation* and *inward investment*.

interlocking spur is one of a series of ridges (i.e. spurs) protruding out from
alternate sides of a river valley. The river will wind around the foot of each
spur. They are more common in the upper courses of rivers.

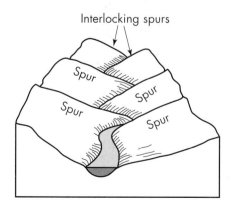

Interlocking spurs

intermediate technology is another name for *appropriate technology* i.e.
technology which is appropriately matched to the needs and skills of less
economically developed countries (LEDCs).

intermittent: a term used to describe:
- a STREAM which flows for only part of the year e.g. during winter in southern Spain or during a wet spell on the chalk downlands of southern England
- a farming system in which land is either not cultivated every year and left
to rest or lie fallow during some years (i.e intermittent cropping e.g. bush-
fallowing in the Central African bush) or continuously in use and perhaps
regularly fertilised with several crops a year being produced (i.e. multi-
cropping and intermittent harvesting).

intrusive is the term used to describe lava or magma (i.e. molten rock)
which is ejected into and hardens within the rocks forming the Earth's crust.
Intrusions such as *dykes* and *sills* affect the landscape either:
- immediately by, for example, buckling up the ground or
- eventually when they become exposed because the overlying rocks have
been eroded.
(See *extrusive*.)

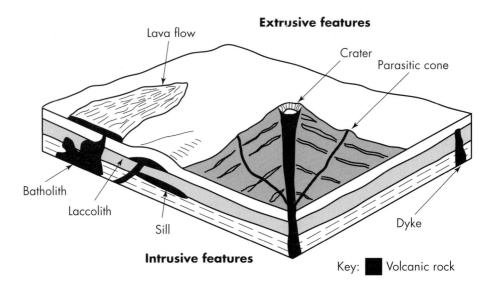

inversion: when the temperature of the air rises with increased altitude (i.e.
height). Normally, temperature decreases with increased altitude.
Temperature inversions can occur in the early morning in valleys after a
cold, cloudless winter's evening. (See *anticyclone* and *lapse rate*.)

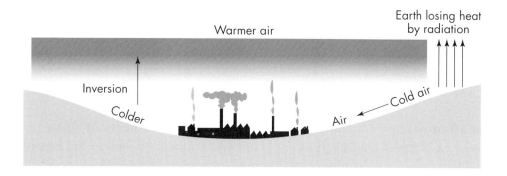

invisibles: trade in services e.g. banking, insurance and tourism, including:
- those services sold overseas (e.g. foreign ships insured in a country) as invisible exports.
- those services purchased from overseas (e.g. tourist visits abroad) as invisible imports;

These are an important part of total world trade, and particularly important to Britain; we usually earn more from invisible exports than invisible imports. (See *balance of trade*.)

inward investment: the capital invested in a region or country from another region or country e.g. a Korean electronics company investing in a factory in Britain or capital from northern Italy being invested in a road or shipyard in southern Italy.

irrigation: the watering of agricultural land by people rather than by rainfall. It is necessary for growing crops in areas of low rainfall. Water stored in the Aswan High Dam and distributed by *channels* to fields irrigates the dry areas in Egypt's Nile Valley. Some British farmers find it necessary to irrigate their fields in summer.

isopleth (or isoline): a line drawn on a map joining places of equal value of a certain factor for instance:
- isobar joins places of equal atmospheric pressure
- isohyet joins places of equal rainfall
- isotherm joins places of equal temperature.

J

jet stream: a very strong wind in the upper atmosphere at about 10 km above the Earth's surface. It blows in a wave-like pattern around the Earth and any change in the pattern of the four main jet streams influences the weather in the atmosphere below.

joint: a vertical crack in a rock caused by natural events. Limestone and granite are very jointed rocks. *Weathering* processes use these joints as lines of weakness to begin the break up of the rock. (See *karst*.)

karst: the type of landscape and scenery found in areas of *carboniferous limestone* e.g. the karst region of Croatia and the White Peak of Derbyshire. Distinctive features can be found:

- on the surface e.g. *gorges*, pavements and swallow holes
- underground e.g. caverns, *pot holes* and underground streams.

Limestone is both *permeable* and soluble in rainwater. Water passes underground and dissolves the limestone on its travels. (See *solution*.)

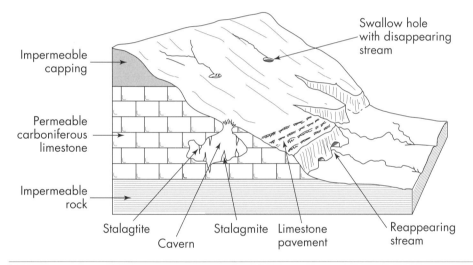

key: an explanation of all the symbols, abbreviations, colours and shadings used on a map or diagram so that it is comprehensive yet not cluttered. A key is an essential part of a good map.

knickpoint: a break of slope in the long profile of a river bed. *Waterfalls* or rapids are often found at this point. They are likely to have been caused by changes in land and sea level. The river downstream of the knickpoint has started cutting down further into its bed. It has been rejuvenated. (See *rejuvenation*.)

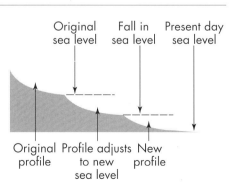

labour-intensive: used to describe an industry which employs a lot of labour in relation to the other *factors of production* – land (raw materials), capital and knowledge. Labour refers to the workforce which can be divided into:

- skilled (e.g. electronics production) or unskilled (e.g. refuse collection)
- manual (e.g. brick-laying) or non-manual (e.g. office work).

Industries in *less economically developed countries* (LEDCs) are often labour-intensive with those in MEDCs such as Japan becoming less so.

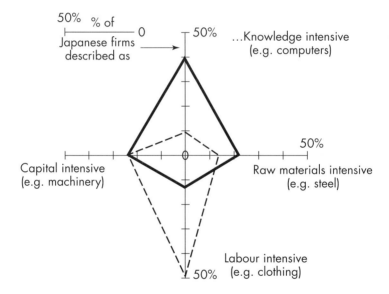

lag time: the time-gap before river *discharge* responds to a change in rainfall. It is shown on a *hydrograph* as the time between peak rainfall and peak discharge. Most rainfall takes time as either *run-off* or *throughflow* to reach the river's *channel*; little of it falls directly into the river. (See *hydrograph*.)

lagoon: an area of shallow sea water along a *coastline* which is partly or completely cut off from the sea by either:

- a spit
- a bar or
- a coral reef.

landfill: a large hollow in the ground into which waste is dumped. Old quarries are often used as landfill sites.

landform: a physical feature on the Earth's surface e.g. a valley.

land consolidation: the knitting together of fragmented land or scattered farms into one unit under a common owner. Large farms may have resulted from consolidation in the past e.g. the enclosure of British farms or the formation of collective farms in China. (See *land reform*.)

land reclamation: the process of turning land which is under water into dry, useable ground. The Dutch have increased the area of their country by reclaiming land from under the North Sea. The reclaimed areas of Holland are known as *polders*. Marshy ground can also be reclaimed.

land reform: a change in land ownership. It has normally involved the sharing out of farmland among peasants and agricultural workers. In the Mezzogiorno region of southern Italy the Italian Government bought land from a few large land-owners before redistributing it in smaller holdings for farm workers to own. Generally, land reform has helped to raise food production in *less economically developed countries* (LEDCs). (See land *consolidation*.)

landslide: a rapid downslope movement of a large body of soil and/or rock either because it has been:
- saturated by water and so has become unstable
- undercut by erosion at the bottom of the slope and so lacks support.
(See *mass movement*.)

land use: the way in which people use land. In towns/cities certain areas generally have a particular type of land use e.g. expensive housing industry. These are known as land use zones or *functional zones*.

land value: the cost of buying or renting land. In towns/cities land values are generally highest in the centre. There is a general decline in land value away from the town/city but small peaks appear at important crossroad areas and near suburban shopping centres. (See *peak land value point / intersection – (PLVI)*.)

lapse rate: the decrease in temperature with height in the lower atmosphere. The general decrease is about 0.6°C. for every 100 metres but the rate at which rising air cools depends upon how much water vapour it contains. Dry air cools more quickly than this, and wet air more slowly. (See *inversion*.)

latitude: the location of a place on the globe in relation to the Equator. Lines of latitude are drawn on maps parallel to, and north and south of the Equator (0°). The North and South Poles have latitudes of 90° N and S respectively. (See *longitude*.)

lava: *magma* or molten rock ejected on to the Earth's surface from below. It is one of the main materials thrown out by active *volcanoes*. Lava flows can be from volcanic cones and from fissures or cracks in the Earth's surface in volcanic areas. Two types of lava are:
- acid
- basic.

(See *acid lava, basic lava* and *extrusive*.)

leaching: the washing out of minerals as water moves down through a soil. It is an important process in the formation of *horizons* in soil. Minerals in wetter climates are washed out of the upper horizons to be deposited in lower ones e.g. *podsols* in the British climate.

leeward: a location facing away from the direction in which a wind is blowing e.g. on the side of a hill sheltered from the wind – the 'downwind' side. In Britain with its prevailing westerly winds the leeward side of the Pennines is the eastern one. Leeward slopes are generally drier than *windward* ones. (See *rainshadow*.)

less economically developed country (LEDC): a country with a low national income *gross domestic product / gross national product* (GDP/GNP) per person, and a general lack of resources, especially financial. LEDCs have large primary sectors because agriculture is still the main type of economic activity. They have a poor standard of living and the general quality of life in them for their people will be low. It is difficult to raise the level of human welfare and quality of life without the wealth to do so. Indicators such as *life expectancy*, the *infant mortality rate* and the *literacy rate* are usually also low in these countries. (See *Brandt Report*.)

levee: a naturally raised bank of mud (*alluvium*) at the side of a river. They are formed by deposition during flooding, and can build up sufficiently to make the river higher than the surrounding countryside. This happens along the *flood plain* of the Mississippi.

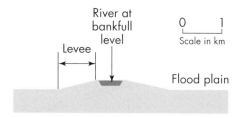

life expectancy: the average number of years a new-born baby can expect to live. It varies:
- from country to country, generally being higher in *more economically developed countries* (MEDCs) than *less economically developed countries* (LEDCs) e.g. at present 75 in Britain and 54 in Tanzania
- over time in a country e.g. a century ago it was about 48 in Britain.

Improvements in life expectancy come with a fall in the *death rate* and *infant mortality rate*, and are due to:
- advances in medicine and health care
- improved housing and sanitation
- better diet and nutrition.

Life expectancy does also vary between the sexes and between different areas of a country.

light industry: the production of goods which are light in weight and often:
- relatively high in value
- small
- easy to transport by road or air
- quite clean and non-polluting.

Light industries produce consumer goods such as clothing and electronic goods. They are often located on *industrial estates* and employ both male and female workers. See *heavy industry*.

limestone is a sedimentary rock which is *permeable*, soluble and contains fossils. There are many different types e.g. carboniferous limestone. See *karst*.

linear: used to describe a long, narrow area of building, often along a road. This can be either:
- a whole settlement, usually a village or
- development in a part of a larger settlement – ribbon or linear development occurs along the main roads in and out of many towns.

(See *nucleated* and *urban sprawl*.)

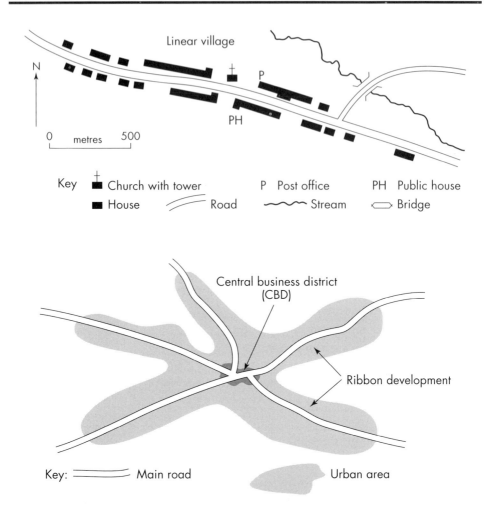

literacy rate: the percentage, usually of the adult population, who are able to read and write. It varies:

- from country to country, generally being higher in *more economically developed countries* (MEDCs) (e.g. 99% in Britain) than *less economically developed countries* (LEDCs) (e.g. 66% in Tanzania), and
- over time in a country, in the last century in Britain it was at the level to be found in several LEDC African countries today.

It is affected by the provision of schooling and is generally used as a *development* indicator, and as a way of trying to measure *quality of life* in a country.

load: the naturally occurring material transported by a river, a glacier or the sea. The amount of load varies according to:

- its availability
- the carrying power of the moving water or ice.

A river's load varies from fine sediment to large boulders, and is greatest when it is fast flowing and during flooding. The load may be in *solution*, in *suspension* or jumping/rolling along the bed of the *channel*.

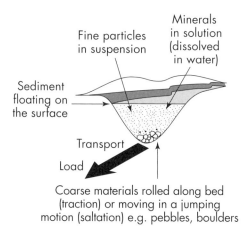

localisation: the concentration of firms in the same industry in one area. It has the same meaning as *agglomeration*. Localised or agglomerated industries are concentrated in one locality.

location: the place at which something can be found. Locations can be described as either:
- absolute i.e. details of the exact place – the land on which a settlement is actually built is known as its *site*.
- relative i.e. its position in relation to other places – the relationship that a settlement has with its surrounding area is known as its situation.
(See *site and situation*.)

loess: soil that has formed from wind-blown dust. The dust has been blown out of either:
- *deserts* (e.g. in the Hwang Ho valley, northern China from the Gobi desert) or
- *periglacial* areas where it was deposited by glacial *meltwater* streams (e.g. in northern France)

longitude: the angular distance of a point on the Earth's surface from the Prime or Greenwich Meridian (0°). On a map it is shown as circles joining the North and South Poles. Longitude is used:
- along with *latitude* to give a place's location
- to define the world's time zones.

long profile: a section of a feature from its beginning to its end e.g. a river valley from its source to mouth.

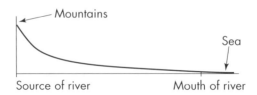

longshore drift: the process by which beach material is moved along a coastline by the waves. When waves break at an angle to the *coastline* as the south-westerly waves do along the English south coast, material moves in a zig-zag fashion along the coastline because of the effects of *swash* and *backwash*. Longshore drift:

● is responsible for the formation of *spits*

● requires groynes to be built if some beaches are not to be lost.

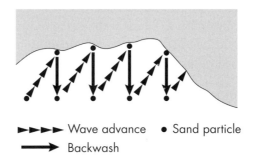

low: another name for a *depression* or a cell of low atmospheric pressure. Lows are associated with cloud, rain and unsettled weather.

low order: any settlement, good or service which is low down its hierarchy.

● A low-order good or service is regularly demanded by people and frequently used or bought. *Convenience goods* such as bread are low order. They are available in most places and people do not travel far regularly to use or buy them (a small *range*).

● A low-order settlement will be small, perhaps a village, and provide probably only low-order goods and services. It will have a small *sphere of influence*.

magma: the molten rock below the Earth's crust. It can:
- force its way into the crust to produce *intrusive* volcanic features
- make its way directly on to the Earth's surface to produce some of the *extrusive* volcanic features – it then becomes known as *lava*. Igneous rocks are formed from magma.

(See *extrusive, intrusive, acid lava* and *basic lava*.)

---

malnutrition: a condition in people which occurs when their diet is insufficient and/or unhealthy.
- short of food i.e. they are *undernourished* or
- short of the right nutrients e.g. vitamins or proteins.

(See *starvation*.)

---

mantle: the layer of the Earth below the crust. It is made of *magma*.

---

manufacturing: the making of goods, usually in a factory by either:
- assembling components e.g. motor cars or
- processing raw materials e.g. aluminium cans.

It is also known as secondary industry or the secondary sector, and has been declining in importance in *more economically developed countries* (MEDCs) in recent times. (See *de-industrialisation* and *sectors*.)

---

marine/maritime: are terms used to describe a geographical factor connected with the sea. For example:
- marine *erosion* or *deposition* is that on a *coastline* by the sea, especially the waves
- maritime air or climate is strongly influenced by the sea e.g. moderate temperatures, humid air and higher rainfall – most of Britain has a maritime *climate*.

---

market: the demand for a good or service backed up by the means and willingness to pay for it i.e. money. Paying customers are the market. Some activities choose a market-orientated location e.g. breweries and bakeries. They locate close to their market or customers.

---

market gardening: farming concerned with the production for sale of fruit, flowers and vegetables. Before recent improvements in transport and food freezing, this type of farming or gardening only took place close to its market i.e. cities and large towns. Nowadays, more distant areas are able to market garden e.g. British supermarkets sell fruit and vegetables from all over the world. Market gardening is:
- *capital-intensive* and
- *labour-intensive.*

In the USA it is known as *truck farming*.

market town: a type of settlement with:
- a weekly or more frequent market, usually of street stalls authorised by royal charter
- a population of small town size e.g. 5,000 to 20,000
- a surrounding rural environment
- little manufacturing industry
- a range of functions e.g. many and various shops, several banks, a hospital.

Retford in Nottinghamshire and Melton Mowbray in Leicestershire are market towns. Some towns which are advertised as market towns may be better described as industrial towns.

mass movement: the movement downslope, under the influence of gravity, of loose materials produced by *weathering*. There are four types:
- Creep – fine and moist materials e.g. some soils move very slowly but fairly continuously.
- Flow – a mass of material can gradually slip downhill.
- Slide – whole sections of a slope can occasionally become detached and slide rapidly downhill as a slab.
- Fall – rocks can fall very rapidly down a slope.

Materials can become unstable and move either because they have been lubricated by water or have been left unsupported below by a slope being undercut at its base. Mass movement is a most important landscape process and occurs on most slopes.

mass production is the manufacture of identical goods in large quantities, using set methods at low average costs.

Mass produced goods such as computers are generally produced in an assembly line factory. Workers specialise on a part of the assembly process. *Mechanisation,* including robots, is used and the parts to be assembled are bought in bulk.

material-orientation: describes an industry which has located near to the source of the raw materials it uses. Brickworks generally locate close to clay pits and sugar beet factories locate in agricultural areas specialising in sugar beet (e.g. Newark, Nottinghamshire). Transport costs are saved as the bulky clay and sugar beet do not need to be transported very far. Bricks and sugar (the finished products) are cheaper to transport because they are not as bulky. (See *market-orientation*.)

maximum–minimum thermometer: one that records the highest (maximum) and lowest (minimum) temperatures over a certain period of time, often a day. Six's maximum and minimum thermometer is a U-shaped tube. The maximum and minimum temperatures are recorded by metal pins. When a set of temperatures has been read, the pins are repositioned using a magnet.

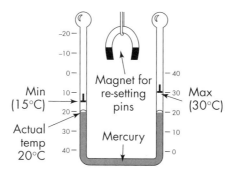

meander: a bend in a river *channel*. Winding courses are a common feature of rivers all along their course. They are more likely to be larger further downstream. Meanders are a changing feature; with *erosion* on one bank and *deposition* on the other the whole feature gradually changes its shape and position.

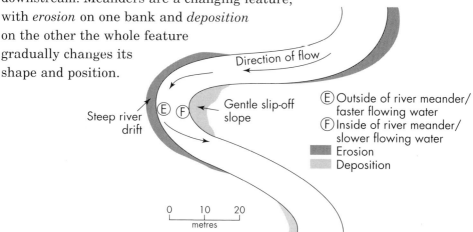

mechanical weathering: the break up of rock by the physical prising apart of the separate particles. Two common ways in which rocks physically disintegrate are:
- by *freeze-thaw* – when water in cracks turns to ice it expands by 9% and forces the crack open; this is also known as frost shattering.
- by exfoliation – repeated heating and cooling of rock causes it to expand, then contract; this can lead to layers of it peeling off – such onion-skin *weathering* occurs in hot deserts

(See *exfoliation* and *physical weathering*.)

mechanisation is the replacement of labour by capital in the form of machinery, for instance:
- robots taking over from workers on an assembly line in a car factory
- computers replacing cashiers in a bank
- combine harvesters replacing farm workers with scythes in a corn field.

(See *automation*.)

Mediterranean: the sea between southern Europe, North Africa and the Middle East which has given its name to:
- a type of *climate* which has hot, dry summers and warm, damp winters
- a type of *vegetation* growing naturally in this type of climate.

Natural Mediterranean vegetation is evergreen woodland (e.g. pine, cypress and cork oak trees) and scrub (i.e. small, stunted trees and bushes which flower in the spring). There is naturally very little grass. The vegetation is adapted to the heat and drought of the summer. Not all plants now growing in Mediterranean lands are natural to that climate; some have been introduced by people.

Mediterranean climates and vegetation can be found in:
- countries around the Mediterranean Sea e.g. Greece, eastern and southern Spain.
- California, central Chile, southern Australia and southern South Africa.

megalopolis: a largely continuous built-up area of over ten million people. Bosnwash in north-east USA is an example. They form by cities and *conurbations* merging together.

meltwater is water from melting snow and ice, usually in glacial areas. It can be found at:
- the base and sides of a glacier where it aids lubrication of the glacier's flow
- the end of a glacier where meltwater streams transport and later deposit material.

These are known as fluvio-glacial features, and are common in *periglacial* areas. Meltwater is strongest during spring and summer, and was important during the *Ice Age* in Britain. It can be seen around glaciers in the glaciated parts of today's world e.g. the Alps. (See *glaciation*.)

mental map: a map that exists in a person's mind. It may well differ from:
- mental map of an area:
- reality
- other people's mental map of that area.

A mental map suggests how a person 'sees' the world.

metamorphic: a type of rock which has been altered from an earlier one by heat and/or pressure. For example, marble is a metamorphic rock which was once limestone, a sedimentary rock. Metamorphic rocks are tough and resistant to *erosion*, and are often used as building materials e.g. slate.

micro-climate: the *climate* of a very small area e.g. the front garden of a house. This micro-climate can be quite different from that in the house's back garden. Micro-climates are very important in farming and gardening; the grower's micro-climatic conditions are those that the crops and plants experience. (See *weather*.)

mid-ocean ridge is an underwater mountain range rising from the ocean bed. The Mid-Atlantic Ridge, for example, runs for 14,000 km along the middle of the Atlantic Ocean. Iceland is one of the high peaks of this volcanic ridge or mountain range. Such ridges are *constructive plate boundaries*.

migration: the movement of people to change their home. Migration, and natural increase/decrease, are the two basic causes of any population change. The types of migration are named after the source area of people on the move (i.e. where the migrants come from) and destination (i.e. where they are going to), for instance:
- rural-to-urban migration is when migrants move from rural to urban areas
- urban-to-urban migration is when migrants move between urban areas
- urban-to rural migration is when migrants leave urban areas for the countryside
- international migration is migrating from one country to another.

(See *push and pull model*.)

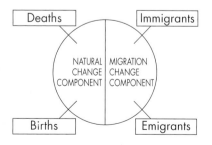

TOTAL POPULATION

million-city is a city with a population of more than one million. There are a growing number of these. There are now more such cities in less economically developed countries (LEDCs) than more economically developed countries (MEDCs) and more than 20% of the world's population live in them. Many of these cities are multi million cities e.g. Seoul, South Korea with 10.6 million. They are also sometimes known as millionaire cities. (See *migration* (rural-to-urban migration) and *urbanisation*.)

mineral extraction is the removal by mining, quarrying or open-casting of economically valuable substances such as iron ore, crude oil or coal from the Earth's crust. Minerals are the inorganic constituents of rocks. They are:
- *primary products*
- an example of the *factor of production* called land
- non-renewable

Their extraction can be environmentally damaging e.g. *limestone* quarries in the Peak District National Park, and the mining villages that grew up on British coalfields during the 19th century. (See *non-renewable* and *primary product*.)

mist is low cloud acting as light fog. It cuts down visibility i.e. the distance you can see, to between one and two km. The condensation of water vapour in the air in the lower atmosphere leads to mist forming. (See *condensation, dewpoint* and *fog*.)

mixed farming: farming which mixes *arable* farming (i.e. the growing of crops) with *pastoral* farming (i.e. the rearing of livestock). A mixed farm combines crop and animal production e.g. animals provide natural field manure and crops are grown as winter fodder for the animals. Many British farms are still mixed to some extent though not necessarily 50:50. The rise of *monoculture* has resulted in the decline of mixed farming in *more economically developed countries* (MEDCs).

model: a simplified generalisation of some aspect of the very complicated world we live in. A model is usually shown as a diagram and focuses on the relationship between a few key factors e.g. urban models show how distance from the city centre can affect *land use*. They give a general guide to what might happen, and can be tested in real places by means of fieldwork. (See *urban structure* (models) and *Von Thunen model*.)

monoculture: farming devoted entirely to growing one crop, for instance:
- coffee, tea, rubber and banana plantations in *less economically developed countries* (LEDCs)

- vineyards in *Mediterranean* climates
- cereal farms on the Canadian Prairies.

Agribusiness makes monoculture more likely as some farmers use high-tech and specialisation on one crop only to chase high yields and profits. Monoculture does have its drawbacks:

- it risks a drop in prices for that crop
- it relies on pests, disease and bad weather not affecting the crop
- it relies on artificial fertilisers to prevent monoculture from ruining the soil.

monsoon: a wind which shifts its direction between the seasons. A good example is between winter and summer in India and South-East Asia. In summer a sea wind brings the heavy rainfall, often thought of as the monsoon (e.g. Cherrapunji, India with over 11,000 mm/430 inches – the wettest place on the Earth). In winter the wind over India changes direction and a dry wind comes from the land.

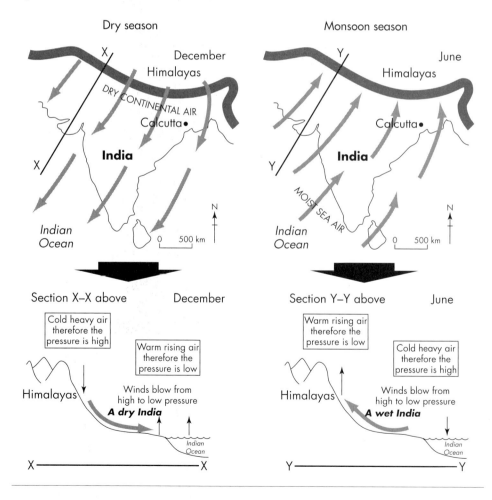

moraine: the stoney debris left behind by the melting ice of a *glacier*. This debris would either have been previously eroded from the land over which it passed or have fallen onto the glacier. Several types of moraine are recognised.

● Lateral moraine – a mound of moraine at the sides of a *glaciated* valley
● Medial moraine – a mound of moraine running down the centre of a valley where two valleys meet. Two lateral moraines join to form a medial moraine.
● Terminal moraine – a mound of moraine at the end of a glacier where it was melting.
● Ground moraine – moraine which accumulates beneath the ice on the valley floor.

Moraine is also known as *till* or *boulder clay*. Some lakes in glaciated areas are dammed by terminal moraines.

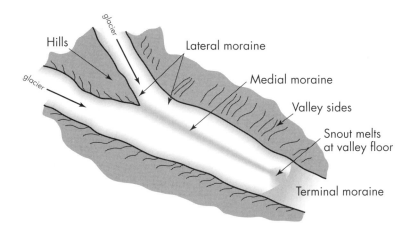

MEDC (more economically developed country): a country with a higher *gross domestic product/gross national product* (GNP/GDP) per person, level of resources and standard of living. These wealthier countries are found in western Europe, North America, Australasia and parts of Asia e.g. Japan. Generally, their greater *wealth* has enabled them to improve the *quality of life* and welfare of most of their populations. Various indicators e.g. *life expectancy*, *infant mortality*, *literacy rate*, have improved as the countries have developed economically. (See *Brandt Report* and *human welfare*.)

morphology: the shape and structure (make up) of a feature, for instance:
● a city as in urban morphology
● a landform as in geomorphology.

mouth: the point at which a river enters the sea. Wide river mouths are known as estuaries. At the mouth of a river fresh water and sea water mix, and sea tides will affect the river's level. (See *source*.)

multi-cultural is a term used to describe a country, a society/community, area or any group which includes people from various different ethnic, racial, religious, language or cultural backgrounds. Migration into Britain from southern Asia (e.g. India, Pakistan, Bangladesh), Hong Kong, the West Indies, other parts of Europe etc. has made Britain a multi-cultural/multi-racial society. There has been some adoption of the cultural customs and habits of newcomers by the rest of the population, and some integration of these people into the ways of the country. A 'new' Britain is being created by this mixing of cultures from around the world.

multi-national company (MNC): a large international firm operating across national boundaries, often in dozens of countries, and exerting enormous influence. Some locate factories in *less economically developed countries* (LEDCs) where labour is cheap and *markets* may be large. Some people think that their presence in these countries is a mixed blessing e.g. they bring jobs but have little concern for what is best for the country's long-term development. They are also known as *transnational corporations* (TNCs).

multiplier effect: the idea that an increase in investment in an area e.g. building a new factory increases incomes in the area by more than the amount of the original investment. If, for instance, the multiplier is 4 then a £100 million investment in a region of Britain by a Korean company will raise incomes in the region by £400 million. This works by increasing local employment and spending: a cycle of growth is set up. (See *cycle of growth/decline*.)

multi-purpose is the term used to describe river schemes which have several aims. Over the past 40 years the Tennessee Valley Project in the USA has had four basic aims/purposes. It has attempted to manage the river Tennessee and its tributaries so that:
- flooding is controlled
- soil erosion is checked and soil conserved
- hydro-electric power is generated
- navigation and river transport are improved.

This is a multi-purpose river scheme set up to try to stimulate one of the more economically depressed areas of the USA. Supplying more water for domestic and irrigation purposes is a further aim of some multi-purpose river schemes. Building dams is generally a key part of any multi-purpose scheme.

national grid has two meanings.
- The series of coordinates used by the Ordnance Survey in Britain. All OS maps fit into a national grid which is printed on the back of the folded 1:50000 sheets.
- The network of *power stations*, pylons, cables and switching centres which generate and distribute electricity in a country. A grid allows high demand in one area to be met by surplus power generated in another.

(See *grid reference*.)

national park is rural land set aside so that its special environment can be preserved for public enjoyment, especially for those people living in urban areas. British National Parks were planned in 1949. There are now 13 e.g. Peak District, Lake District, Brecon Beacons, Norfolk Broads, which cover about 20% of England and Wales, and over half of the upland areas of the two countries. There are National Parks in other countries e.g. Yellowstone in the USA and part of Amazonia in Brazil. There are controls on new development in National Parks, for instance:
- new buildings have to be made of the same stone, and to the same design, as older buildings
- permission for industries such as quarries to open is difficult to obtain
- new roads are either diverted around the Park or hidden in tunnels without cuttings.

Combining public access with conserving outstanding natural environment is a difficult task for a National Park authority. Conflicts of interest about the way in which land in National Parks should be used are common e.g. the congestion at a tourist *honeypot*, while satisfying the need for public access for city people, may conflict with the need to conserve the land-scape and with the rights of local people to get on with their lives in peace and quiet.

natural gas occurs naturally in the Earth's crust, often close to crude oil. The natural gas found beneath the North Sea and Morecambe Bay has become a major source of energy in Britain, for use in both homes and *power stations*, and has largely replaced gas made from, for example, coal. The so-called 'dash for gas' is a dash for natural gas. It is:
- *non-renewable, fossil fuel*
- cheap and straightforward to store
- transportable by pipeline.

natural hazard: the threat to life and property posed by an aspect of nature. *Earthquakes*, blizzards, *drought* and *hurricanes* are natural hazards. They can become natural disasters when the threat becomes an event. Earthquakes threaten life and property in California but when one actually occurs the destruction can prove to be a disaster. Such events are expected in some places but they can rarely be accurately predicted. Natural hazards have their greatest effect in *less economically developed countries* (LRDCs) and in urban areas. (See *human hazards*.)

natural increase: an increase in population caused by the *birth rate* exceeding the *death rate*. The other basic cause of population increase is *migration* change. Rates of natural increase vary from country to country and from time to time. At present, natural increase is highest in *less economically developed countries* (LRDCs) where death rates are falling yet birth rates remain high. (See *demographic transition model*.)

natural resource: a gift of nature e.g. land, forests, minerals, which is of use to people. Natural resources are also known as land, and are one of the four *factors of production*.

natural vegetation: the kind of *vegetation* which would grow naturally in a place without the influence of people. In most parts of the world the natural vegetation has been modified by human activity. Mixed woodland is the natural vegetation of most of England. (See *Mediterranean*.)

neighbourhood: a distinctive area within a town or city in which:
- the residents are known to each other
- there are amenities for the local residents e.g. church, pub, primary school, convenience shops.

New towns in Britain have been planned on the basis of neighbourhood units in order to give people a sense of belonging to a community. Each unit has housing, amenities to serve local family needs and is bounded by roads.

neo-colonialism: the influence which some *more economically developed countries* (MRDCs) have over some *less economically developed countries* (LRDCs). The influence is of an old colonial power and MEDC, such as Britain, on LEDCs which were once former colonies e.g. West Indian islands. Such former colonies may now be independent countries but MEDC influence persists because old trade patterns continue. *Multi-national companies* based in the MEDC are often involved in and benefit considerably from this trade e.g. in bananas.

network: a connecting pattern or system of roads, railways, rivers or canals. Goods, services, people, money or information flow through networks which are made up of:
- *nodes* i.e. places or junctions such as towns
- links i.e. routes such as roads to one another.

New Town is a town which has been:
- newly created
- centrally planned
- built as a whole
- built on a *greenfield site* or around an existing settlement.

In Britain, New Towns were built to:
- relieve overcrowding and congestion, especially in London (e.g. Stevenage, Crawley)
- counteract decline and unemployment in the old industrial areas (e.g. Peterlee, Skelmersdale).

They have been laid out with:
- a regular street pattern
- modern industrial estates on the outskirts
- self-contained *neighbourhood* units.

newly industrialising country (NIC): a country which until quite recently was a *less economically developed country* (LRDC) but is now experiencing rapid industrialisation. The best examples are the so-called 'five tiger economies' of South Korea, Hong Kong, Singapore, Taiwan and Malaysia where the following have grown rapidly:
- *manufacturing industry*
- cheap *exports*
- incomes and *gross domestic product/gross national product* (GDP/GNP) per person
- *multi-national companies*

● environmental *pollution*.
(See *Pacific Rim*.)

---

node is a place where a transport *network* can be joined e.g. a town or junction (i.e. meeting place) of routeways. Towns often developed at nodal points where routes met.

---

nomadic pastoralism: a type of farming in which people wander from place to place living on milk and meat from their cattle, sheep or camels. It takes place in arid/semi-arid regions such as the deserts of North Africa and the Middle East and involves a constant search for fresh pasture for grazing. It has declined in recent times because:
● there is concern about the environmental damage caused by overgrazing land that is already little vegetated
● governments now often stop nomads from crossing national boundaries
● there is less open public land available to nomads.

---

non-renewable: a natural resource which once used, cannot be replaced (it is exhaustible) e.g. coal, oil, natural gas, iron ore. A large proportion of the world's electricity comes from the use of non-renewable resources. (See *fossil fuel* and *renewable resource*.)

---

nuclear power is the power released by splitting the nucleus (i.e. inner core) of uranium or plutonium atoms. 70% of France's electricity is generated in nuclear *power stations*. There are health and safety concerns associated with nuclear power stations, and such stations in Britain have generally been located on remote coastlines. However, nuclear power stations do not release gases into the atmosphere which cause *acid rain* or contribute to the *greenhouse effect*.

---

nucleated: a settlement where the buildings are grouped or clustered around a central point or nucleus e.g. a market square, village green or cross-roads. (See *linear settlement*.)

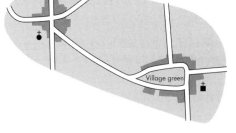

occlusion: a *front* which is a combination of a *cold front* and a *warm front*. This is the final stage of a frontal *depression*. The cold front catches up with the warm front, and pushes the warm sector upwards. Occluded fronts bring cloud and rain.

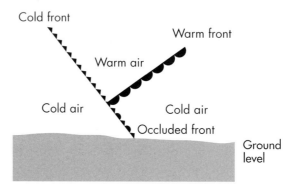

ocean current: a stream of water which is
- warmer or colder
- faster flowing

than the surrounding ocean. The Gulf Stream and North Atlantic Drift are warm currents and play a big part in keeping the North Atlantic Ocean and its nearby countries such as Britain relatively warm in winter. The El Nino Effect is the occasional change in the Peru Current from cold to warm. Ocean currents have a major influence over *weather* and *climate* on land.

ocean trench: a long, narrow and very deep gorge in the ocean floor. Trenches are found:
- at *destructive plate boundaries* where one plate sinks beneath another
- around the edge of the Pacific Ocean.

The Mariana Trench off Japan is over 11,000 metres deep and the deepest sea bed in the world.

offshore bar: a ridge of shingle slightly out to sea and not connected to the land. A bar might form across the mouth of a river or the entrance to a bay, and become a shallower area of sea near the coast which may be uncovered at low tide. *Bars* are often washed landwards by the waves.

opencast mining is the extraction of minerals from the surface of the Earth; sinking shafts or boring tunnels is not therefore necessary, as it is in underground mining. Iron ore, phosphates and some coal are extracted by opencasting. Coal was removed from the site of Sheffield City Airport in the 1990s before the runway was concreted. Opencast mining sites are now generally landscaped when mining operations cease.

optimum population: the ideal size of population for that area, or country's, other resources. *Standards of living* will be highest when this number of people occupy the area or country. Areas which are either overpopulated or underpopulated are so in relation to their optimum or ideal size; i.e. too many or too few people for the other resources and technology available. (See *overpopulation* and *underpopulation*.)

order of good/service: describes the frequency with which goods are used or bought.
● Low order – everyday sort of goods and services which may be bought at least once weekly e.g. popular foods or the post office. They are to be found in almost all settlements and need only a low *threshold population* to exist.
● Middle order – goods and services used and bought a few times a month e.g. a tape/CD store or cinema. They are supplied only in towns and cities.
● High order – goods and services used and bought infrequently e.g. a concert hall or a formal dress agency. They have a high threshold population and can be found only in major towns and cities.

ordinary business district (OBD): a large suburban shopping centre in a city. In general an OBD will:
● serve a large district of the city
● provide *convenience goods* (e.g. a supermarket, bakers), some specialist consumer goods (e.g. dresses, carpets), a few chain stores (e.g. Boots) and some personal services (e.g. bank, building society)
● be one of a small number of such centres in most cities
● be located where roads to and from the city centre cross roads running around the city
● have been an old village centre before *urban sprawl* overran the village.
Some OBDs in very large cities have as many shops with as great a range as in the central business district (CBD) of a town e.g. 100-plus shops.

Key:

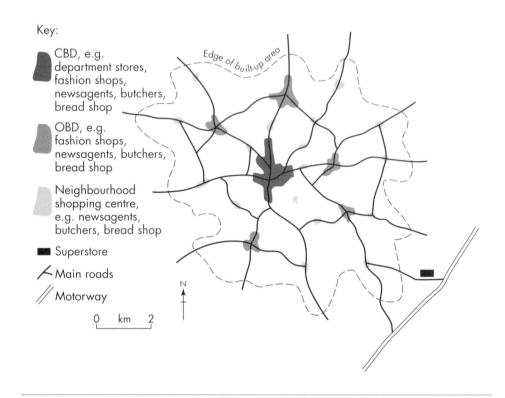

CBD, e.g. department stores, fashion shops, newsagents, butchers, bread shop

OBD, e.g. fashion shops, newsagents, butchers, bread shop

Neighbourhood shopping centre, e.g. newsagents, butchers, bread shop

■ Superstore

⟨ Main roads

// Motorway

0 km 2

organic farming: farming without the use of artificial chemicals such as:

- fertilisers
- pesticides
- growth stimulants.

Instead, naturally occurring materials and traditional *labour-intensive* approaches to farming are used. Environmental *pollution* is reduced but organic food prices are higher.

orographic rain is rain caused by high relief. It is also known as *relief rainfall*.

out-migration: the permanent movement of people outward from one place in a country to another in the same country. For example, with urban-to-rural *migration* in present-day Britain there is out-migration from a town or city. (See *emigration*.)

out-of-town location: a site on the edge of a town/city which is relatively open and rural. Land on this *rural-urban fringe* has recently become very popular for *superstores*, high-tech industries, shopping and leisure complexes because:

- there is space for building and car parks
- there may be good access and little road congestion for car owners
- land may be cheaper than in many other parts of the city.

(See *greenfield site*.)

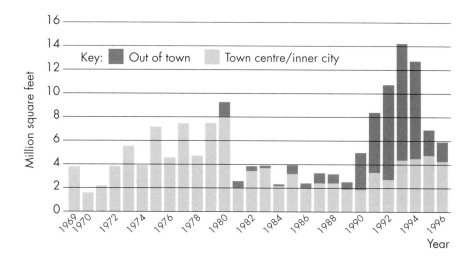

output is production. Production requires inputs into the production process i.e. of land, labour, capital and knowledge (*factors of production*). (See *system*.)

outward investment: capital (money) leaving a region or country to be invested in another e.g. a Canadian company investing Canadian money in a hotel, business or building, or both, in the West Indies. There will be outward investment in Canada but inward investment in the West Indies.

overcrowding: the state in which too many people or living organisms are present for the space available. In Britain an overcrowded house is one where there are more people living in it than there are rooms other than the kitchen and bathroom, e.g. a six-roomed house with four bedrooms, a lounge and a dining room will not be overcrowded until it has at least seven residents. Overcrowded houses are one indicator of *deprivation*.

overgrazing: the loss of grass and other vegetation from an area because too many animals, especially cattle and sheep, are grazed on it. The exposure of the soil will lead to it being eroded, and can result in the area becoming a *desert*. This has been happening in the *Sahel* area of central Africa where the Sahara Desert has spread further southwards. (See *desertification*.)

overpopulation: describes the state in which too many people are present in a region or country for the available resources to provide for everyone. A reduction in the number of people in an overpopulated region or country would lead to a rise in living standards. China is generally believed to be overpopulated in relation to its *optimum population*, and has been adopting family planning policies in an attempt to reduce its total population.

overproduction: when the supply of a good by industry or agriculture exceeds the demand for it. There is a surplus at the going price for the good. *Food surpluses* e.g. 'butter mountains' and 'olive oil lakes' have been a feature of agricultural production in the *European Union* countries. (See *Common Agricultural Policy (CAP).*)

overspill: that part of the population of a large town or city which has moved to areas outside the settlement to find more space or better living conditions. Some *New Towns* have been built to meet this overspill e.g. London overspill in Stevenage and Harlow.

owner-occupier: someone who lives in and owns their own house. Owner-occupation is one of the main types of housing tenure in Britain.

ox-bow lake: a small curved lake which was originally a river *meander*. They are found on a *flood plain* alongside a meandering river. Ox-bows or cut-offs are formed when a meandering river straightens its course by cutting through the land between a meander. The old course is left as a lake until it dries out and becomes reclaimed by vegetation.

ozone layer: a layer of gas in the upper atmosphere. This layer is made up of a type of oxygen, known as ozone, which filters ultra-violet short-wave radiation from the sun. This protects life on the Earth from radiation damage. Ozone in the lower atmosphere is an air pollutant and 'greenhouse gas'. In recent times, holes in the ozone layer over the North and South Poles have been discovered. These are thought to be due to the emission of chlorofluorocarbons (CFCs) from artificial products e.g. aerosol sprays and refrigerators.

Pacific Rim: the countries around the Pacific Ocean. Those in the West Pacific Rim (e.g. Japan, Taiwan, South Korea, Hong Kong, Singapore) have developed to form a major industrial area. This development is known as the *global shift*. Most of these countries are *newly industrialising countries* (NICs).

Pacific Ring of Fire: the *volcano* and *earthquake* belt located at, or relatively near, the edge of the Pacific. Many of the world's most active volcanoes (e.g. Krakatoa in Indonesia and Pinatubo in the Philippines) and most destructive earthquakes (e.g. San Francisco and Kobe, Japan) occur in this belt. It exists because the oceanic *plates* under the Pacific sink and subduct where they meet the continental plates of Asia and the Americas. *Destructive plate boundaries* occur around the Pacific Rim. (See *subduction*.)

Key: ━━━━━━━ Pacific Ring of Fire

parallel drainage: a river system in which the *channels* run almost parallel to each other.

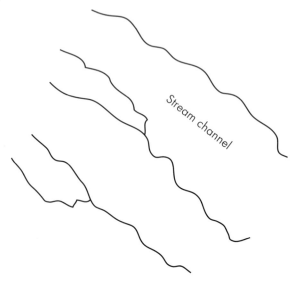

Stream channel

parasitic cone: a smaller cone which develops on the side of the main cone of a volcano. Mt Etna on Sicily has hundreds of parasitic cones whose *lava*, ash and other volcanic material comes from the main cone's vent. (See *composite volcano*.)

park-and-ride: a scheme to try to reduce town/city centre traffic congestion. Car parking space is provided, often free of charge, towards the edge of the town/city. A frequent bus service running from the car parking area transports people into the *central business district* (CBD). This service may also be free of charge. York and Oxford operate such schemes.

pastoral: a type of farming concerned with the rearing of livestock e.g. cattle or sheep for their meat or products such as milk, wool or hide.

peak flow: the maximum amount of river *discharge* shown on a *hydrograph*, normally after a storm.

peak land value point/intersection (PLVI): the place within a town/city where land values are highest. It usually occurs at a major intersection within the *central business district* (CBD) e.g. a corner where two main (perhaps pedestrianised) shopping streets meet. Pedestrian counts will be high at this point, and high-profile shops such as Marks & Spencer and large department stores are likely to be located here.

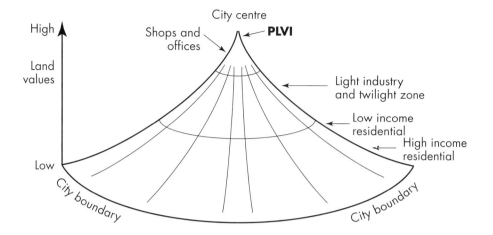

High

Land values

Low

City centre

Shops and offices

← **PLVI**

Light industry and twilight zone

Low income residential

High income residential

City boundary

City boundary

pedestrianisation: a scheme to reduce traffic congestion by closing a road/street to vehicles. This is now common in many town/city centres. Pedestrians are the sole users of a pedestrianised area although service vehicles such as buses and taxis are sometimes allowed access.

percolation: the process by which water moves downwards through soil and *permeable* rock. This seepage down through the ground follows *infiltration* into the ground surface. (See *hydrological cycle* and *water table.*)

periglacial: the area bordering a glaciated one. At the perimeter (border) of an *ice sheet* the land will not actually be covered by ice but will:
● be frozen for quite a depth (i.e. *permafrost*) e.g. 3–4 metres
● thaw in the top few centimetres in summer
● have *meltwater* from the ice flowing over it.
The Siberian and Alaskan *tundra* today is a periglacial area. During the *Ice Age* in Britain the ice sheets reached a line joining London to Bristol – at this time southern England was therefore a periglacial area. (See *glaciation.*)

periphery: the area away from the economic core i.e. the area of greatest economic activity and development. (See *core* and *periphery.*)

permafrost: present when the soil and rock below the surface layer remains permanently frozen for at least two years. Permafrost occurs under *periglacial* conditions. Ground affected by permafrost is poorly drained and difficult to build on.

permeable: a property of rock which allows water to pass through. Rocks can be permeable if they are:
- *porous* – contain pores such as *chalk*
- pervious – made up of cracks and joints such as *limestone*.

Permeable rocks rarely have any surface drainage. This lack of streams and rivers reduces the amount of *erosion* suffered by these rocks, and helps to explain why they often form higher ground.

physical geography: that area of the subject of geography which studies natural environment e.g. *weather* and *climate, soils, landforms.* It is difficult to divorce the study of people from physical geography as they affect the natural environment as well as being affected by it.

physical weathering: another term for *mechanical weathering.* Rocks can be physically prised apart by weathering processes.

pie-graph/chart: a circle divided into sectors or wedges. Each sector is proportional in size to the value it represents. The North line (0°) is the starting point. The sectors are marked in a clockwise direction in a descending order of size with the largest value first.

plain: a level area of land at low altitude. Plains are the most common type of land surface on the Earth covering about 30% of the surface. They are often grasslands.

planning is part of the work of the local authority (e.g. city council, county council) and concerns the use to which land can be put. Local authorities regulate new building development in order to:
- ensure it is in the best interests of the area
- try to minimise conflicts within the community.

Planning permission or planning restrictions can be granted, governing a wide range of land uses.

plantation: a large tropical/sub-tropical farm or estate which:
- practices monoculture
- is commercial and often owned by a *multi-national company*
- usually produces tree or bush crops e.g. rubber or tea
- employs a large labour force.

Plantations were set up in tropical countries e.g. Nigeria, Kenya, Malaysia in the old colonial days.

plate (tectonic plate): a large, rigid slab of the Earth's crust. The crust is divided into a number of these gigantic slabs, up to 100 km thick, which float like rafts on the Earth's molten *mantle* beneath. There are:

- Oceanic plates made of heavy rocks
- thicker Continental plates with lighter rocks on top.

It is at the boundaries or margins of these plates that major *earthquakes, volcanoes* and rock *folding* occurs. (See *destructive plate boundary* and *constructive plate boundary*.)

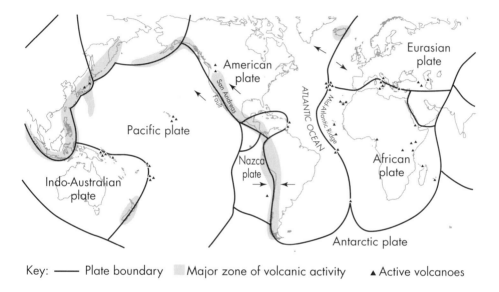

Key: —— Plate boundary ▓ Major zone of volcanic activity ▲ Active volcanoes

---

plateau: a level area of land higher than its surroundings, often in an upland area e.g. the Massif Central, France.

---

plucking: the pulling of surface fragments off a rock which has become frozen to the ice. Such fragments are plucked away when the glacier moves. It is a type of glacial erosion. It occurs in a *corrie* and may explain the jagged rock surface forming the backwall of the corrie.

---

plunge pool: the deep pool at the bottom of a *waterfall*. The force of the falling water and its load of boulders and other materials erode this pool in the river bed (i.e. *hydraulic action*).

---

podsol: the most common type of soil in Britain and the result of podsolisation or *leaching* i.e. the downward movement of water and minerals through the soil. Rainfall is greater than evaporation. A typical podsol profile is shown on the next page.

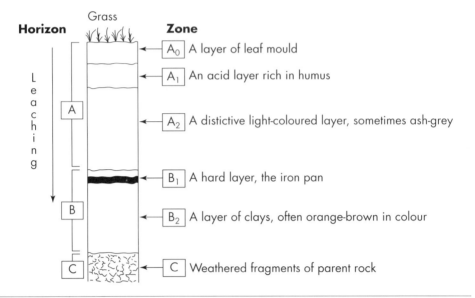

polder: the Dutch name for land reclaimed from the sea. Polderland in Holland supports both agricultural and urban/industrial use. Reclaiming this land from the sea involves building a dam, known as a *dyke*, across a coastal inlet, pumping out the seawater and removing the salt from the polderland if it is to be used for *arable* farming. In 1932 the Zuider Zee in Holland was dammed to keep out the North Sea and create the Ijsselmeer polders. Similar schemes have taken place elsewhere in Holland since. Together they have:

- increased the land area of Holland.
- protected the country from flooding by North Sea storms.

If *global warming* does raise the level of the sea by a metre worldwide, coastal protection will be necessary. (See *reclamation*.)

pollution: a change for the worse inflicted on the natural environment by human activities. This environmental change usually takes the form of chemical contamination by industry, traffic or agriculture of:

- land
- air
- water.

Pollutants can be:

- biodegradable e.g. sewage – they may be harmful and unattractive at the time of pollution but do not necessarily cause any permanent damage
- non-biodegradable e.g. lead – these can cause more permanent pollution damage by, for example, entering the food chain and being passed from organism to organism.

Acid rain, 'holes' in the *ozone layer*, and any *global warming* are the result of air pollution. The air can also be polluted by noise, and ugly buildings can cause visual pollution of the land.

pool: a deep section of a river bed. (See *riffle*.)

population density: the number of people living in an average square kilometre. (See *density of population*.)

population distribution: the characteristics of the spread of population over an area. Distributions are often studied by plotting *population densities* on a map. Population is unevenly distributed because of differences in:
- *relief*
- *climate*
- *soils* and vegetation
- water supply
- mineral resources and energy supply
- transport and communications.

The Earth's *hostile environments*, and most of the world, are sparsely populated. Population clusters in some very densely populated regions e.g. South east Asia and California.

population explosion: the rapid increase in the world's population that has occurred during the 20th century. Most of this explosion is now taking place in the *less economically developed countries* (LEDCs). Natural increase, due to *death rates* falling more than *birth rates*, has been significant in these countries. Family planning and population control policies have been introduced in some countries. (See *demographic transition model*.)

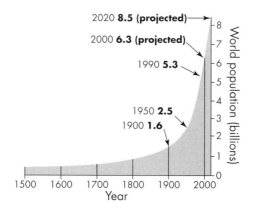

population pyramid: a diagram to show the age and sex structure of a population. This data is represented:

- as horizontal bars
- with males on the right and females on the left
- in intervals of five years e.g. 0–4, 5–9 year olds
- with the youngest at the bottom and oldest at the top.

When drawn for a *less economically developed country* (LEDC) or a traditional society such as 18th century Britain, the diagram has a pyramidal shape i.e. the older the age group the fewer there are of that age. This occurs when *birth rates* are high and *life expectancy* low. The shape of the diagram reflects changes in the birth rate and the *death rate*. At present *more economically developed countries* (MEDCs) have population pyramids that more clearly resemble cylinders, or even onions, than pyramids. (See *ageing population*.)

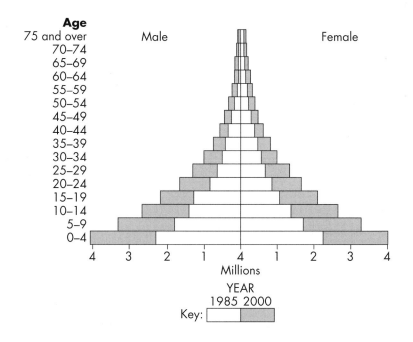

population structure: the make-up of a population by age and by sex (gender). *Population pyramids* are drawn to show population structure.

population transition model: another name for the *demographic transition model*.

porous rock contains a large number of small air spaces or pores e.g. *chalk*. Most porous rocks are *permeable*. The pores generally allow water to pass through.

positive discrimination: a policy which favours more disadvantaged and deprived groups or areas in order to offer equality of opportunity. Job recruitment policies can, for instance, favour:
- the physically disabled
- ethnic minorities
- women
- the long-term unemployed.

Job applications from these sections of the community can be encouraged or targets set for the proportion of these groups represented in a company's workforce. Positive discrimination policies can be used to try to boost declining regions or depressed inner city areas. Special treatment can be afforded to people and companies working in those locations.

post-industrial society/country: one in which:
- old heavy *manufacturing* industry has declined i.e. *de-industrialisation*
- *service* industries are the key type of industry
- information technology is dominant
- there is a large professional and technical labour force.

The USA and Britain are examples.

pothole: a term which describes either:
- a small fairly circular hollow in the rocky bed of a river – formed by *corrasion* (abrasion), and most common in the river's upper course or
- a large vertical hole in limestone not used by a stream – formed by *solution* of the joints in the rock.

(See *karst* and *carboniferous limestone*.)

power station: an electricity generation plant. It produces electricity from various *primary* energy sources:
- thermal power stations burn *fossil fuels* e.g. coal, natural gas
- *nuclear power* stations split uranium or plutonium atoms
- alternative power stations harness water or tidal power.

Power stations are linked with environmental issues(e.g. air *pollution* and *acid rain* from thermal stations) and health and safety issues (e.g. radioactive leaks from nuclear stations).

prairie: a flat area of natural grassland named after the central plain of the USA and Canada. Large areas of the North American prairie grow cereals. The term prairiefication is now used to describe the changes in the British countryside in areas like East Anglia which have produced:
- fairly flat *arable* land

- large fields
- lack of hedges.

The removal of hedgerows is a cause of conflict between some farmers and food companies, and those groups concerned about landscape *conservation*.

precipitation: the collective name for all the moisture, in its many forms, that reaches the Earth's surface for instance:

- *rainfall*
- *snow*, hail and sleet
- *fog* and *mist*
- dew and frost.

All these forms of precipitation are originally caused by moist air rising and, as a result, cooling below its *dewpoint* temperature. (See *humidity*.)

pressure (air): the weight of a column of air on the Earth's surface. This weight is the result of gravity and decreases with height. Average air pressure at sea level is taken as 1,000 millibars though this does vary from place to place and from time to time at the same place. There are two main types of occurrence of high and low pressure.

- Fairly permanent belts of high or low pressure at some locations on the globe e.g. the Azores High at the *Tropic* of Cancer, and the Icelandic Low at the Arctic Circle. These belts drive the major wind systems of the world e.g. the south westerlies over Britain.
- Temporary cells of high pressure (i.e. *anticyclones*) or low pressure (i.e. *depressions*) which are carried along in these wind systems. They affect the weather of the places over which they pass for short periods.

prevailing wind: the most common wind direction at a particular place. In Britain the prevailing winds are west/south west. (See *wind rose*.)

primary is a term used in a number of contexts in geography.

- Primary data – original information collected first-hand by fieldwork.
- Primary industry – involves obtaining raw materials from *extractive industries* (e.g. mining) and other primary products from agriculture and fishing.
- Primary *sector* – includes all the primary industries in a country/economy. In *less economically developed countries* (LEDCs) this sector employs a larger proportion of the labour force than the *secondary*, *tertiary* and *quaternary* sectors.
- Primary energy – includes the basic energy sources (i.e. coal, oil, solar power) which can be converted into secondary energy e.g. electricity, petrol.

private sector: that part of a country's economy not owned or controlled by the state e.g. Marks & Spencer, Tesco. The transfer of state-owned (or nationalised) industries into private companies e.g. part of British Rail to Virgin Rail, is known as privatisation.

profile: this term has two meanings.
- Soil profile – a vertical section of soil showing various *horizons* (see *podsol*).
- Landscape/townscape profile – a side view of a feature e.g. a valley or a settlement. Cross-sections or transects are profiles.

protectionism: a government policy towards international trade, protectionism is the imposition of trade barriers at the frontiers of a country. Home industries are thus protected against competition from abroad as the places of *imports* into a country is reduced. This restriction of imports can be achieved by:
- setting an import quota – allowing only a fixed amount of, say, foreign cars to be imported
- charging a tariff or import duty at Customs on all or some imports – this may make imports more expensive than home-produced goods.

Governments can also try to protect their *exports*, but generally they are encouraged to favour free trade between countries rather than self-protection.

public sector: that part of a country's economy owned and controlled by the state e.g. the National Health Service and local authority education. In Britain the size of the public sector has shrunk since the early 1980s as privatisation has occurred. (See *private sector*.)

push-and-pull model: a way of explaining population *migration*. The model points out that people move in response to being 'pushed out' of a place (i.e. push factors such as poverty) and/or being 'pulled into' another place (i.e. pull factors such as better educational opportunities).

pyramidal peak: a sharp, pointed mountain peak formed by glacial erosion. During a glacial period e.g. the *Ice Age*, three or more *corries* were eroded back-to-back on a mountain side. These had the effect of sharpening the original mountain peak so that it came to resemble a peak at the top of a pyramid. The Matterhorn in the Swiss Alps is a pyramidal peak (see *glaciation* and *glacial trough*.)

pyroclast: a solid object e.g. solidified *lava*, thrown out of a *volcano* during an eruption. (See *extrusive vulcanicity*.)

quadrat: a metal, usually square, frame used during fieldwork. It is a means of sampling the ground e.g. the kind of vegetation growing in the area of a randomly placed metre square quadrat.

quality of life: a term describing the level of people's total well-being and happiness. There have been various attempts to try to put a value on this for ordinary people. A true value will include the *standard of living* and all the other indicators of people's *wealth* and welfare. The quality of people's lives depends on *gross domestic product / gross national product* (GNP/GDP) per person, medical matters such as *life expectancy* and the rate of *infant mortality*, educational matters like the adult *literacy rate*, diet matters like the calorie consumption per day, environmental matters such as air *pollution* and the amount of open space, and many more. The attempts to measure this key idea have involved using an index i.e. a combination of indicators put together to give a final 'score' for a country. (See *development* and *human welfare*.)

quarrying is the extraction of rock and any minerals it contains from large surface workings. Many quarries are large excavated hollows. *Limestone*, *chalk* and sandstone are quarried.

quaternary: this term has two meanings.
- The geological period in which we live. It started about three million years ago with the onset of the *Ice Age*. This first glacial phase of the Quaternary is called the Pleistocene. The more recent phase since the Ice Age is known as the Holocene.
- A fourth and modern sector of work in an economy. The quaternary sector covers activities offering advice, training, research, development and support to other services in the *tertiary sector* e.g. a computer consultant, a barrister. This sector is very much larger in *more economically developed countries* (MEDCs) than *less economically developed countries* (LEDCs).

quota: a fixed amount of a good or service that can be:
- produced e.g. milk in the *European Union* (EU) countries
- traded e.g. foreign cars imported into Japan.

Quotas have to be set by a government or other powerful body in order to be effective. (See *protectionism*.)

radial drainage: a pattern created by river or stream *channels*. The channels flow or radiate out from a central high point such as a mountain. The Lake District has radial drainage as the rivers flow away from this upland in all directions.

radiation is energy in the form of heat given off by a warm object. There are two main natural sources of radiation.
- The Sun – the amount of heat energy from the Sun which reaches the Earth's surface is called *insolation* or solar radiation. This is only a fraction of what it emits. Much is lost because it is either reflected, absorbed or scattered by the *atmosphere* and *clouds*.
- The Earth – the ground heats the atmosphere above it by re-radiating heat energy previously received from the Sun. This radiation is known as ground or terrestrial radiation. It has a different wave-length to solar radiation.

Differences in radiation between day and night, the seasons and places has a significant effect on climate e.g. solar radiation is greatest at the Equator where temperatures are high and least at the Poles where temperatures are low.

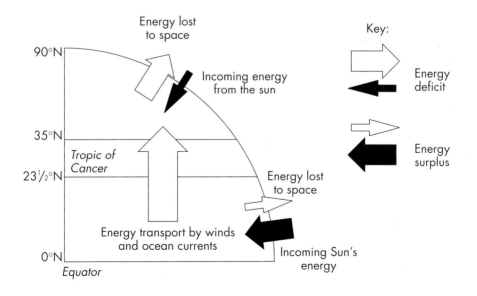

radiation fog is that due to loss of heat from the ground by *radiation* during the night. Clear skies and calm conditions are ideal for radiation *fog* to form. (See *anticyclone*.)

rainfall is made up of water droplets large enough to fall from *clouds* onto the Earth's surface. It is the principal type of *precipitation*, and results from the cooling of rising air. The air's ability to hold moisture depends chiefly on its temperature. When rising air cools, it can hold less; any surplus condenses out as cloud. Rain is made in some clouds when further *condensation* forms tiny water droplets; these can join together. There are three types of rainfall, each type being named after the way in which air is forced to rise.
- *Relief rainfall* – high relief e.g. mountains pushing moving air upwards.
- *Frontal rainfall* – air rising at the *fronts* in a depression or cyclone.
- *Convectional rainfall* – warm air rising because it is lighter.
(See *convection* and *depression*.)

rainforest is dense forest, mostly found in tropical *latitudes* where the climate is hot and wet throughout the year. (See *tropical rainforest*.)

rain gauge: an instrument consisting of a funnel, cylinder and collecting bottle used to measure *precipitation*, usually *rainfall*. Measurement is daily in millimetres.

rainshadow: the area of relatively low *rainfall* on the *leeward* side of a mountain range. The leeward side is the slope sheltered from the winds which bring rainfall to:
- the windward side
- the mountain tops.
On the leeward side the air:
- is descending and so becoming warmer and dryer
- has already lost some of its water content as it rose over the mountains earlier.
Rainshadows exist in areas of *relief rainfall* e.g. the eastern side of the Pennines.

raised beach: a beach or platform once formed by the sea but now standing above the present sea level. A drop in sea level or a rise in land level are responsible for its formation. Raised beaches are part of an old, now dry, *emergent coastline*. Examples can be found around the *Mediterranean* coastline i.e. in Cyprus, Malta.

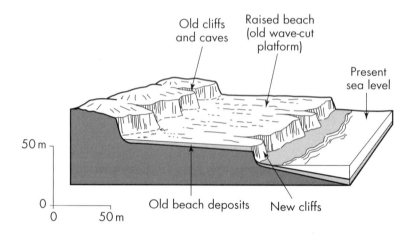

Old cliffs and caves

Raised beach (old wave-cut platform)

Present sea level

50 m

0

0   50 m

Old beach deposits   New cliffs

ranching: the grazing of cattle or sheep on very large farms i.e. ranches. The animals graze on:
- natural pasture as well as fodder provided by the ranchers
- land enclosed by fences as well on open land where they roam freely.

Ranching is at the same time *extensive, commercial* and *pastoral farming*. A good example are the estancias on the Pampas grasslands of Argentina. (See *fodder crop*.)

range has three meanings in GCSE geography:
- In settlement studies, range is the maximum distance that people will travel to buy a particular good or use a particular service. Each good and service has a range. For example, to use a theatre people may be prepared to travel, say 30–40 km, whereas to buy a magazine from a newsagent their range for travel may be only 1–2 km. The higher the order of a good/service the greater is likely to be its range. A *desire line* drawn on a map shows the range for that good/service.
- In climatic studies, range is the difference between the highest and lowest measurement, usually of temperature. Temperature ranges within a day and within the year are frequently calculated. The annual temperature range is the difference between a January temperature and a July temperature. This meaning of range is the one that applies to the term tidal range – the difference between high tide and low tide.
- A chain of mountains can also be described as a range. For example, the Andes mountain range in South America.

rapids are small waterfalls and stretches of rough water along a river. They generally form where thin bands of weak rock alternate with thin bands of hard rock along the bed of a river *channel*. Examples can be found along the upper stretches of the river Nile.

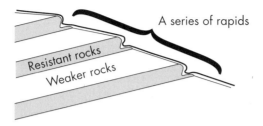

A series of rapids

Resistant rocks

Weaker rocks

---

rapid transit system: the arrangements for transporting large numbers of people quickly around a big city. The idea is to avoid traffic congestion and the use of cars. The system in Vancouver, Canada involves light rail cars powered by electro-magnets running along steel rails:
- underground
- on the ground
- and above the ground.

The London Underground and Sheffield's Supertram are rapid transit systems.

---

raw material: any substance which can be processed to make an industrial or food product. Raw materials such as timber, wheat, crude oil, etc. are *primary* products, which are *inputs* into *secondary* or *manufacturing* industry. The source of raw materials is an important factor in some industrial locations, especially old heavy industry.

---

reclamation: the process of making previously unusable land available for agriculture, leisure or building. The land concerned may originally have been:
- beneath the sea e.g. the Dutch *polders*
- marshland e.g. the new tourist areas in Languedoc, southern France, once coastal marshes
- derelict e.g. the Don Valley Stadium, Meadowhall Centre and Sheffield Arena, on reclaimed built, derelict industrial land.

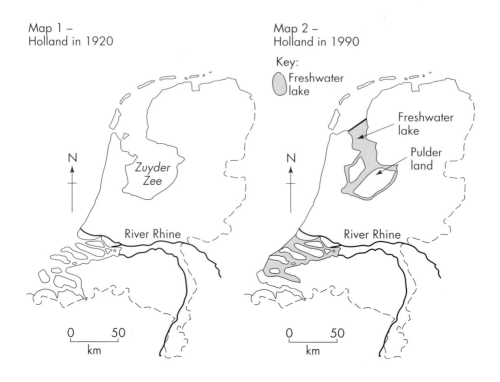

Map 1 –
Holland in 1920

Map 2 –
Holland in 1990

Key:
Freshwater lake

Freshwater lake

Pulder land

N

N

Zuyder Zee

River Rhine

River Rhine

0   50
km

0   50
km

---

recreation is any leisure activity that does not involve an overnight stay. Examples include a local fishing trip and an afternoon countryside hike.

---

recycling is the re-use of resources. It involves the processing for re-use of waste glass, paper, some scrap metals, etc. from:
- factories
- homes.

Recycling helps to:
- save scarce resources, especially *non-renewable* ones
- reduce environmental *pollution* e.g. cuts down on waste disposal by *landfill*.

Roughly 20% of a new BMW car is made of recycled resources. Most local authorities in Britain operate voluntary recycling schemes for household waste.

---

redevelopment: fundamental alteration of the characteristics of an area. This usually involves the knocking down of houses and other buildings, and the construction of new ones and/or roads on the same site. Such schemes have been common in Britain over the past 50 years in:

- city centres/*central business districts* (CBDs) where increasing traffic congestion has led to pedestrianised streets, wide inner relief roads, tramways, etc. being created
- old inner city areas where poor quality housing is in need of replacing.

refugee: a person who flees from their homeland to escape from danger or persecution. They are forced migrants seeking refuge in another country from:
- war
- political unrest
- disasters such as drought and famine.

The United Nations calculation is that there are 17 million refugees in the world. Probably the best known are the Palestinian refugees living outside Israel in various Middle East countries e.g. Syria, Lebanon.

region: an area of the Earth's surface with features which distinguish it from other areas around it. It is one of the five *spatial* scales of geography:
- global
- international
- national
- regional
- local.

Amazonia is an example of a regional scale; the region is a natural one and has a special physical geography. The East Midlands is an economic region within the United Kingdom.

regional imbalance: this term describes the idea that there are differences in economic development between the various *regions* of a country, for instance:
- in the rate of unemployment
- in wage/salary levels
- in house prices.

In Britain unemployment is around 11% in Merseyside but nearer 5% in South-East England. These differences:
- are known as the regional problem
- occur in all countries
- vary as time goes on – in Victorian times Merseyside was a booming area with lower unemployment than many other regions
- lead to governments having a regional development policy which attempts to keep the differences to a minimum.

rejuvenation: the increase or re-start of a river's downward *erosion*. It often occurs when *base level* drops because:
- sea level falls or
- land level rises.

Rejuvenated rivers develop a new *profile* and features such as *waterfalls* at *knickpoints*.

relative humidity: a measurement of the amount of moisture or *water vapour* in the air. It is given as a percentage of the maximum amount of water vapour that air could hold at that temperature. The relative *humidity* of saturated air is 100%.

relative poverty: a condition in which people are badly off compared with others in the same society. In modern Britain those without a car or unable to afford a holiday can argue relative poverty even though they do not lack basic needs such as food or clothing. (See *absolute poverty*.)

relief: the shape of the Earth's surface. This normally includes its altitude or height. Relief is shown by the *contours* on an Ordnance Survey map.

relief rainfall: rainfall caused by high *relief*. Hills and mountains force air to rise. As it rises it cools and becomes unable to carry as much moisture as before. Temperature falls with height and warm air can hold more moisture than cold. *Cloud* and rain can form as a result of this rising and cooling of air.

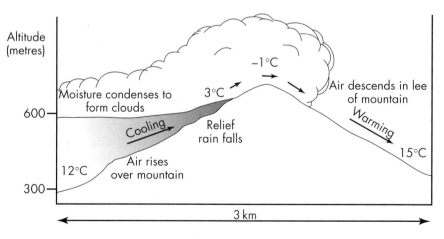

renewable resource: a resource such as energy which will not run out, or its source of supply become exhausted, because:
- the supply is endless e.g. wind energy
- it can be grown e.g. timber.

If supplies of the second type do begin to run low then it is possible in time to replace them. For example, salmon supplies can be renewed by salmon farming in Scottish lochs. Resource management might try to avoid the need for replacement or renewal by seeing that resource use is never greater than present supply. Renewable energy sources such as solar panels, wind farms and tidal barrages now supply more electricity worldwide than they did 30 years ago.

reservoir: a lake, usually artificial although it can be natural, used for collecting and storing water. The lake often forms behind a dam and may be used:
- to provide homes and industry with water
- to create hydro-electric power
- to provide water for irrigation
- for leisure activities.

Reservoirs are the main source of water supply in many countries, and are usually built in areas of higher rainfall, often uplands. They enable:
- wetter areas e.g. Lake Vyrnwy, Wales, to supply drier or more populated areas e.g. Birmingham, with water
- water to be stored from the wet season for use in the dry season e.g. the Damodar Valley reservoirs in India save monsoon rain until the dry season.

resettlement: people being moved into homes new to them, often in another area, for example:
- in many British cities people living in *inner city* 'slum' areas have been resettled in outer city estates
- some city authorities in *less economically developed countries* (LRDCs) e.g. Bombay, India have resettled *squatters* from *shanty towns*.

Resettlement policies generally move people into homes with better facilities than they had previously.

residential type: the type of house ownership (or tenure) in an urban area. The three main types are as follows.
- Owner-occupied – residents owning their home.
- Council – residents renting their home from their local council.
- Privately rented – residents renting their home from a private landlord.

These different residential types often segregate people according to the amount that they are willing or able to pay for housing. Council housing can be on estates quite distinct from residential suburbs with large numbers of owner-occupied houses.

resistance: the ability of rock to withstand *weathering* and *erosion*. Hard rock is more resistant to weathering and erosion than soft rock, and often forms higher ground e.g. the *chalk* of South-East England forms *escarpments* in the Downs while softer clay forms the vales. (See *escarpments*.)

resort: a town whose main business is tourism. There are:
- coastal resorts e.g. Blackpool
- ski resorts e.g. Aviemore, Scotland
- lakeside resorts e.g. Bowness-on-Windermere.

Resorts generally have a *tertiary* labour force e.g. waiters or water sport instructors, but may suffer from seasonal unemployment e.g. at ski resorts in summer.

resource: *inputs* into the production of goods and services. They fall into two categories.
- Natural resources e.g. climate, water, territory, mineral deposits. They are also known as land and can be split into *renewable* (e.g. water) and *non-renewable* (e.g. *fossil fuel*) resources.
- Human resources e.g. labour, knowledge and capital (i.e. finance and technology).

Careful management of resources is generally necessary. Sustaining future supplies of, for instance, non-renewable natural resources may require:
- stopping their exploitation
- conserving stocks and reserves
- developing new or alternative supplies.

retail park: a shopping development usually located in an outer town/city area. They usually consist of a number of independent stores each in separate buildings served by one large car park. Most retail parks sell both goods e.g. Currys, Toys R Us and services e.g. Macdonald's-drive-through, and can be found on either:
- *greenfield* (previously countryside) or
- *brownfield* (previously derelict) land.

These parks are one of the more recent developments in retailing; goods and services being sold in this setting away from the *central business district* (CBD).

revetment: a heavy fence, usually of wood or metal, built along a *coastline* to protect it from *erosion* by the sea. Revetments usually slope seawards, and may be part of a number of coastal protection measures e.g. *gabions* or cages

of boulders in front of the revetment. Revetments are less
expensive to build than either sea
walls or a series of *groynes*.

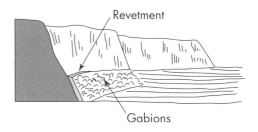

ria: a long, narrow inlet of the sea formed by the flooding of a coastal river
valley. The flooding can be due to either:
- a rise in sea level or
- the sinking of an area of land.
There are several rias in South-West England e.g. the river Fal between
Falmouth and Truro; most are surrounded by hills.

ribbon development: the development of buildings, usually along a road,
can lead to:
- a town or city developing ribbon-shaped *suburbs* spreading out into the
  surrounding countryside
- a village becoming *linear* or ribbon-shaped.

ribbon lake: a long, narrow lake on the floor of a U-shaped glacial valley or
trough. Lake Windermere in the English Lake District is a ribbon lake. They
can form:
- in a rocky hollow carved out by a glacier as it cut the whole valley into a
  U-shape
- behind a mound of debris, perhaps a *moraine* or landslide – water builds
  up on the valley floor behind this barrier.
(See *glacial trough*.)

Richter scale: the main scale used to measure the power of an *earthquake*.
It is named after its designer, Charles Richter, and:
- is open-ended at the top end i.e. it does not have a set maximum
- has a logarithmic scale.
Each full point is ten times more powerful than the previous full point. An
earthquake measuring 6 on the Richter scale is a thousand times, and not
twice as powerful as one measuring 3. The most powerful earthquake so far
recorded measured 8.9 on the Richter Scale.

Magnitude	Description
2.5–3	If nearby, the earthquake can be felt. Each year, there are about 100,000 quakes of this power
4.5	Earthquakes of this power can cause local damage
5	About equal in quantity to the first atomic bomb
6	Destructive within a limited area. About 100 per year of this power
7	1995 Kobe earthquake. Anything of this power and above is a major earthquake and can be recorded over the entire earth; 14 per year of this power and greater
7.8	1906 San Francisco earthquake
8.4	Close to the maximum observed. Examples are Hinshu 1993 and Alaska 1964
8.6	Energy released is three million times that of the first atomic bomb

ridge: this term is used in two ways in geography.
- A long, narrow and steep-sided piece of ground higher than surrounding land. It would normally be of more *resistant* rock.
- A long, narrow area of high atmospheric pressure stretching out from an *anticyclone*. The weather under a ridge of high pressure is the same as that under an anticyclone.

riffle: an area of shallower water in a meandering river. Deposition of material on the bed of the river causes this area of shallower water. (See *meander*.)

rift valley: a steep-sided valley formed between roughly parallel faults. Rift valleys can be found at plate boundaries, especially constructive ones where the crust is being pulled apart causing faults. Land can sink between the faults; the East African Rift Valley is an example. (See *faulting*.)

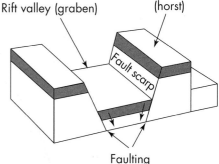

Rift valley (graben)

Block mountain (horst)

Fault scarp

Faulting

river capture: the stealing of one river's water supply by another more active, neighbouring river. The more active or pirate river cuts into the course of its neighbour and intercepts its water. As water becomes diverted the two rivers change their length; the pirate becoming longer and transporting more water while the opposite happens in the other river.

river cliff (or bluff): the steeply sloping bank along the outside of a *meander*. It is formed where the river current is fastest as it sweeps around the outside of the meander. *Erosion* by this fast-flowing water undercuts the outer bank. (See *meander*.)

river management: people's attempts to influence water flow and quality in a river basin in order to:
- reduce *flooding*
- provide *irrigation* water
- enable hydro-electricity to be produced
- provide conditions for leisure pursuits
- reduce *pollution*.

This can involve:
- building dams, locks, sluices, culverts, etc.
- monitoring the weather, river conditions and water demand regularly.

(See *hydro-electric power*.)

river terrace: a level area like a bench or step in a river valley by the side of the *channel*. It is the remains of an old *flood plain*. *Rejuvenation* of the river has increased its power to erode so it has cut through the flood plain, and left a terrace above the present river level. The river Thames has cut terraces in its lower course, which are now occupied by parts of London.

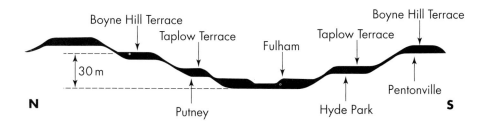

rock: solid, natural material which:
- is made of minerals
- is cemented together
- forms the Earth's crust.

There are three groups of rock.
- *Igneous*
- *Sedimentary*
- *Metamorphic*.

ro-ro (roll-on/roll-off): a sea transport method in which ferries transport loaded vehicles. Lorries, coaches and cars drive on to the ferry at one end and drive off at the end of the crossing. This method:
- saves time and money in loading and unloading cargoes
- requires specially designed ships (e.g. flat-bottomed) and port facilities (e.g. large vehicle parking areas)
- suits shorter sea crossings where loading/unloading costs are relatively expensive.

The ferries from Portsmouth across the English Channel to the French ports of Caen, Le Havre, St Malo and Cherbourg use the ro-ro method.

rotation: has three meanings in GCSE geography.
- In agriculture, rotation is the planting of crops in a sequence. Different crops take different minerals out of the soil and perhaps add different minerals to it. Soil *fertility* can often be best preserved by growing one crop one year, another crop the following year and so on.
- In physical geography, rotation is the turning of the Earth on its own axis. A full rotation takes 24 hours and leads to day and night occurring.
- In another area of physical geography, rotation describes the way a mass of rock, soil or ice slips or slides down a curved slope. The material moves in a semi-circular way.

rough grazing: poor quality grassland used for sheep, goats and, occasionally, beef cattle. Areas used for rough grazing are generally:
- natural grassland, often upland e.g. moorland
- unfenced and open
- unimproved by people.

Sheep farming on the fells of the Lake District can be described as rough grazing.

route: a line of communication, transport or movement. Journeys occur along routes. Routes link places which can become route centres when several routes converge there. Route centres are accessible places, and generally attract industry and population. Motorway junctions in Britain have become route centres which today attract industrial *development*. (See *link* and *node*.)

run-off: the water that flows over the Earth's surface after *rainfall*. It includes:

- channel flow i.e. in rivers and streams
- overland flow i.e. over the rest of the land.

Run-off occurs when rainfall does not either percolate or infiltrate into the ground (e.g. because of very heavy rainfall) or evaporate back into the atmosphere. (See *evaporation*, *hydrological cycle*, *infiltration* and *percolation*.)

rural depopulation: the fall in population of rural (countryside) areas. The main cause is as follows.

- Rural-to-urban migration e.g. people leaving farming, perhaps because of unemployment due to its greater mechanisation, for life in a city where, for example, job prospects may be better. Push and pull factors cause this migration. It has been a feature of most *more economically developed countries* (MEDCs) in the past, and has been happening in many *less economically developed countries* (LEDCs) more recently.

Rural depopulation leaves rural areas short of:

- young labour
- services in villages.

(See *migration*, *push and pull model*.)

rural development: encouraging and assisting rural (countryside) industries and community development in villages and other rural settlements (i.e. *hamlets* and *market towns*). Rural development aims to stop further *rural depopulation*. The opening of food processing plants in the rural areas of *less economically developed countries* (LEDCs), near to the farms that supply them, is an attempt to do this.

rural–urban fringe (rurban): the area of transition between town and countryside. In this area there are both urban (e.g. housing and supermarkets) and rural (e.g. riding schools and garden centres) features, often side by side. The demand for this land is very high in both:

- *less economically developed countries* (LEDCs) e.g. from *squatters* in *shanty towns*.
- *more economically developed countries* (MEDCs) e.g. from house-builders and industrialists looking for *greenfield sites*.

Sahel: an area of semi-desert conditions to the south of the Sahara desert in Africa. It frequently experiences *drought* which causes the desert to expand into the area. *Famine* is often a threat in the Sahel countries e.g. Ethiopia in 1984. (See *desertification*.)

saltation: the bouncing of particles over the Earth's surface. Heavier particles are transported along the bed of a river *channel* in this way. The wind causes sand grains to bounce across a *beach*.

saltmarsh: a saline (i.e. salty) *wetland* along a *coastline*. They usually develop either:
- around a river estuary
- behind a spit.

Their vegetation is specially adapted so as to be able to tolerate salt water. At high tide sea water normally enters the marsh. Saltmarsh can be found along the Lancashire coast between Morecambe and Fleetwood.

satellite image: a picture of the Earth's surface taken from an artificial satellite high in the *atmosphere*. Two common uses are in:
- weather forecasting from cloud cover images
- *land use* mapping.

saturation: the air, soil or rock cannot hold any more water (or *water vapour* in the case of the air). Further cooling of saturated air leads to *condensation*. Further water to saturated ground leads to *flooding*.

savanna: large, open areas of *tropical grassland* found in Africa, South America and northern Australia. Generally, the vegetation includes:
- coarse grass which can be tall
- shrubs, often thorny
- scattered trees with small, flat leaves and again, often thorny.

Savanna vegetation is supported by the savanna type of *climate* which is:
- hot and wet in summer
- warm and very dry in winter.

These conditions suit grass more than trees though there are more trees close to the *rainforest* edge of the savanna, e.g. in Africa on the savanna's southern edge. The safari parks of East Africa e.g. Amboseli, are in savanna areas.

scale: this term has two uses in GCSE geography.
- On a map, scale is the relationship which exists between the map and the ground it represents. A 1:50000 Ordnance Survey map is 50,000 times smaller than the ground it shows. Map scales are indicated as a statement and/or a scale line.
- Scale also describes the size of the area being studied.

Five area scales are recognised:
- small i.e. local studies
- regional e.g. Yorkshire
- national i.e. a whole country
- international i.e. between countries e.g. the *European Union* (EU)
- global i.e. worldwide.

scarp: a slope, usually steep and short. On the *chalk* downlands of southern England a scarp slope and a dip slope form an *escarpment*. In northern England a short, steep *limestone* slope is called a scar. *Faulting* can leave behind a cliff-like slope known as a fault scarp.

scattergraph: a graph which plots the relationship between two factors as a scatter of dots. Adding a trend (or best-fit) line to a scattergraph enables the nature of this relationship to be described and then explained. The scattergraph shown below shows negative correlation: countries with low *gross national product* (GNP) per person have high birth rates. High GNP per person countries have low birth rates. You would be expected to give a geographical explanation for this in an examination.

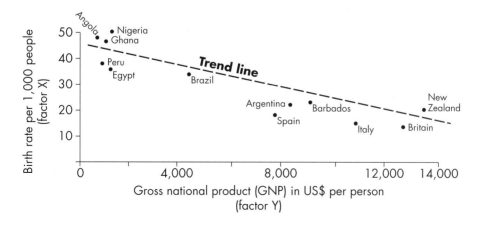

schist: a layered *metamorphic* rock. It was slate which has been altered by heat and pressure in the Earth's crust.

---

science park: a high-tech industrial area, usually near a university. Businesses located in the park generally make electronic, computing and medical products with the help of scientific research and development. There are strong links with the local university e.g. Oxford Science Park. (See *business park* and *technology park*.)

---

scree: rock fragments and small boulders which litter hill slopes, especially towards the foot. They have been formed by:
- *weathering* of the slope face followed by
- movement down the slope under the influence of gravity.

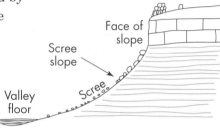

---

sea defences: those attempts to protect the *coastline* from *erosion* and *flooding* by the sea. Sea walls, *groynes*, *revetments*, *gabions* and breakwaters can be built to defend the coastline.

---

sea level: the average level of the sea surface. *Contour heights* in Britain are based on sea level at Newlyn, Cornwall. Sea level can rise or fall in relation to the land. For example, at present:
- there is a fear that *global warming* will melt some of the world's *ice sheets* and glaciers and cause sea level to rise
- sea level around Britain is changing very slowly as the country rises – it had been forced downwards by the weight of the ice during the *Ice Age* and is now recovering.

---

secondary: this term has two uses in GCSE geography.
- Secondary products are finished goods made by secondary or *manufacturing* industry which forms the secondary sector. *Primary* products (e.g. raw materials) are processed in the secondary sector into finished goods.
- Secondary data is information collected by someone other than the user – computer databases, libraries and town halls are sources of secondary data.

second home: a home whose owner lives elsewhere for much of the year (i.e. in a first home). They are often used for recreation during part of the year only e.g. holiday cottages in the Lake District owned by families from Manchester or Sheffield.

sector: a broad category of economic activity. Different industries and jobs fit into one of the four sectors – *primary*, *secondary*, *tertiary* and *quaternary*. The relative size of each sector changes as a country develops economically over time.

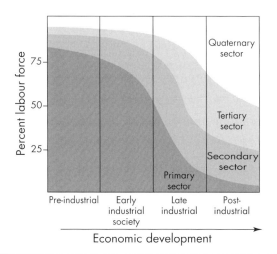

sedentary: describes a farmer who remains settled in one place. There are farming systems which involve movement of the farmer and, perhaps, animals from place to place. (See *nomadic pastoralism*.)

sedimentary: a group of rocks formed from sediments. They:
- have accumulated over long periods, usually under water
- have a layered structure, and are described as stratified
- often contain fossils.
Sandstone, *limestone*, *chalk* and coal are examples.

segregation: where certain groups of people live apart. This situation can either:
- be forced e.g. as in South Africa before apartheid was abandoned or
- come about for economic and social reasons e.g. less well-off people living in an area of council housing; people of the same ethnic origin clustering together in an inner city area. Social and economic segregation is a feature of all towns and cities in Britain. (See *ethnic area*.)

seismograph: an instrument which measures and records seismic, or *earth-quake*, activity. It traces the length and strength of an earthquake on a graph.

self-help scheme: people being encouraged by a project, perhaps set up by government, to help themselves improve their conditions. In some *less eco-nomically developed countries* (LEDCs) money loans and building materials have been provided by government so that *squatters* can develop their *shanty towns* themselves e.g. the Arumbakham self-help scheme in Madras, India.

self-sufficiency: the ability to meet your own needs, especially for food. Britain is largely self-sufficient in a range of foods produced in *temperate* latitudes e.g. potatoes, cereals and sugar beet. British agriculture is able to feed the British population in these foods. Subsistence farmers try to be self-sufficient; they grow only enough for their own eating and clothing needs.

service: this term has two meanings in GCSE geography.
● Service can be used to refer to the *functions* of a settlement. These services are the jobs and facilities that serve the local population e.g. mining, a university. Larger settlements become service centres for a region.
● Service also refers to activities, other than making goods, which improve people's welfare. Service or *tertiary* industries and the service/tertiary *sector* provides services to customers e.g. shops, schools and restaurants.

sere: a series of plant communities. Each community is succeeded by another until a more permanent community develops. The more stable community is known as the climax. The plant succession which starts in fresh water by a lakeside is known as a hydrosere.

set-aside: an agricultural scheme in the *European Union* (EU) countries. It is a voluntary scheme designed to reduce the surplus production of *arable* crops. In return for taking out of production a proportion of their arable land (known as set-aside land), farmers receive annual compensation payments from the EU. If they enter the set-aside scheme, farmers use set-aside land to:
● grow trees
● support certain non-agricultural uses e.g. tourist facilities, camping sites, games pitches, riding schools, game and nature reserves.
Set-aside land can also be left to lie fallow.

shanty town (or spontaneous squatter settlement): an area of unlawful, makeshift housing. This area:

- grows very quickly (spontaneously) because of the high demand for cheap housing
- develops on unoccupied land owned by others – residents become squatters
- is often found on the edge of cities in *less economically developed countries* (LEDCs). There are examples of shanty towns within these cities. Many rural-to-urban migrants, who partly account for the rapid growth of some LEDC. cities, live in shanty towns.

Housing is made from any available cheap material (e.g. packing cases, cardboard); sanitation and supplies of water, gas and electricity often do not exist; overcrowding is common; and roads generally unmade. Some shanty towns have been bulldozed away without warning; in others, attempts have been made to upgrade them. (See *migration* and *rural depopulation*.)

shield: this term has two uses in GCSE geography.
- Shield areas are the very old cores of the continents. The rocks are stable and rigid e.g. the Canadian Shield.
- Shield *volcanoes* are wide, gently sloping volcanic cones. They form from highly fluid (or basic) *lava* which flows readily over some distance before solidifying. Mauna Loa, Hawaii is an example, resembling a flattened shield on its side. (See *basic lava*.)

shifting cultivation: a system of farming used in some of the forested areas of Africa, Asia and South America. The sequence of events are:
- a patch of forest is cleared by slash-and-burn
- crops such as yams and cassava are grown in the small clearing for a few years
- the cultivators move on to clear another patch of forest
- earlier forest clearings are left as bush fallow land – vegetation re-grows and soil regains its fertility.

In 'bush fallowing' the farmers return to earlier clearings without moving home. True shifting cultivation takes place where the farmers move house. Both types of shifting cultivation do little long-term damage to the forest environment.

shopping mall/centre: a covered area, often on more than one level, containing a large number of shops. They can be found either:
- in city/town centres which have been redeveloped and where public transport is good or
- towards the edge of cities/towns where car parking is easy.

The latter can take custom away from city/town centres. (See *redevelopment*.)

sill: a horizontal volcanic intrusion. *Lava* flows along the bedding planes of rocks beneath the surface. It solidifies as a sheet of *igneous* rock and if exposed on the surface by *erosion* of the overlying rocks, can form an *escarpment* e.g. the Great Whin Sill, Northumberland, which has Hadrian's Wall built on it in places. (See *intrusive vulcanicity*.)

silt: a fine-grained sediment forming soil. It is deposited by rivers and running water.

sinuosity: refers to the straightness of a river or stream's *channel*. Channels with a high sinuosity are winding with *meanders*.

site and situation are the two types of location.
- The actual ground on which a settlement or building stands is called its site. This is its absolute location. Early villages were sited where shelter, water, meeting points and defence could be provided. In modern, larger settlements some of these original site factors can usually still be identified e.g. the meeting of valleys, control of routeways and river crossings found at Salisbury.
- A settlement or building's position in relation to other places and features is called its situation. This is its relative location. Settlement situations are often shown by a sketch map which might include close-by settlements, *relief* features, rivers and motorways. Some of these features can, if favourable, lead to the *development* of the settlement.

skills: the tasks you have to undertake as opposed to know or understand. Measuring the velocity of a river or plotting figures on a graph are geographical skills. GCSE coursework tests skills heavily.

slate: a *metamorphic* rock. This type of rock:
- was formed by shales being compressed by natural forces within the Earth's crust
- easily splits along its thin bedding planes
- is a traditional roofing material.

sleet: a mixture of *snow* (or hail) and water.

slum: a low-quality house. This poor housing is often found close to other such houses so the phrase, slum area or slums. In *more economically developed countries* (MEDCs) these areas are usually found in inner cities, and associated not only with deteriorating buildings but with:

- overcrowding
- crime, drugs, prostitution and vandalism
- failing schools
- unemployment and poverty
- poor access to food shops.

Slum clearance schemes have occurred in some parts of British cities over the past 40 years.

slumping: a type of rapid *mass movement*. Weathered material slides down a slope:

- as a mass
- along a curved surface.

Slumps can be seen at the foot of the soft glacial deposit cliffs along the Yorkshire coast.

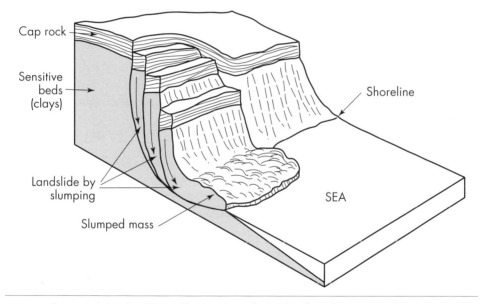

Cap rock

Sensitive beds (clays)

Shoreline

Landslide by slumping

Slumped mass

SEA

smog: fog combined with *pollution* (smoke). Smoke abatement laws were introduced in the urban areas of Britain to prevent pollution from factory and house chimneys turning natural fog into smog. Cities such as Los Angeles and Athens are today famous for petro-chemical smog caused by large amounts of car exhaust pollution.

snow: *precipitation* in a solid state. At temperatures not usually much below freezing point, *water vapour* in the atmosphere can:

- freeze into minute ice crystals
- matt together into a light, white flake, often as it falls towards the ground.

socio-economic: refers to people's income and wealth, occupation and housing. It enables geographers to recognise:
- socio-economic areas – where people of similar socio-economic status congregate
- urban structure – a pattern of *land use*, especially of residential areas within towns/cities based on socio-economic areas e.g. low income residential areas with little owner-occupation close to the *central business district* (CBD).

soil acidity: the concentration of hydrogen ions in soil as indicated by its pH value. Acid soils have a low pH value (i.e. 6 or less) and may be due to:
- shortage of salts from the parent rock
- salts being leached out of the soil by acid *groundwater* from decaying organic matter.

Basic soils have a low acidity and high pH value due to their:
- high salt and lime content
- low organic matter content.

soil conservation: attempts to keep as much of an area's topsoil in place as possible. Soil conservation methods aim to reduce soil *erosion*. Some methods of doing so are:
- planting grasses and trees on steep slopes
- planting shelter belts of trees
- *contour ploughing*
- *terracing*.

soil creep: the slow movement of soil down slopes. It is a gradual but constant process caused by:

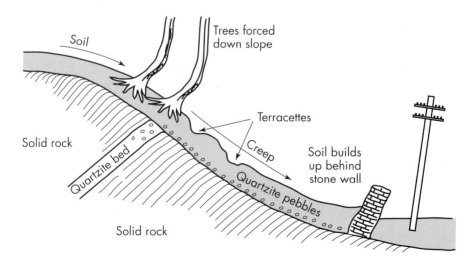

- alternate wetting and drying of the soil
- alternate freezing and thawing of the soil.

It is a major type of *mass movement*.

soil erosion: the removal of topsoil by water, wind and gravity (i.e. *mass movement*). Human activities can either:
- accelerate soil erosion e.g. *overgrazing* exposes bare soil, or
- reduce soil erosion i.e. *soil conservation*.

Six causes of soil erosion are as follows.
- Cutting down trees (deforestation) removes protection for soil.
- Gullies eating into the soil. Heavy rainfall leads to gully erosion.
- Overgrazing, due to too many animals per hectare eating and trampling vegetation.
- Ploughing straight up and down hill. Rainwater flowing downhill in the plough channels causes soil to be washed away.
- River banks crumbling, exposing soil to further erosion.
- Continuous growing of the same crop (monoculture) exhausts the soil, making it more likely to be blown or washed away.

soil profile: the arrangement of the soil in layer-like *horizons* of differing texture, colour and consistency. Soils are recognised and classified into broad groups on the basis of their *profile*. There are three general parts to any soil profile.
- Horizons A and B form the true soil.
- Horizon C forms the subsoil or weathered parent material.
- Horizon D is the parent bedrock.

soil texture: the size of the inorganic particles in soil. Five soil texture groups are recognised.
- Gravel – very large grains.
- Sand – where medium size grains dominate.
- Silt – where fine particles dominate.
- Clay – where very fine particles dominate.
- Loam – a mixture of some of the above types but no one type dominates.

solar: relates to the Sun as a source of heat and light for the Earth. This heat and light is transferred to Earth as waves of solar radiation. This energy source has been utilised for electricity generation in recent times. Solar energy is:
- renewable
- unreliable in many parts of the world.

The generally higher temperatures in *tropical* latitudes is due to the fact that they receive the most solar radiation.

---

solution: the dissolving of some minerals in water (e.g. calcium carbonate). It is a major cause of:
● *erosion* by running water, rivers and the sea
● eroded material being transported by water.
(See *corrosion*.)

---

source: the origin of:
● a stream or river i.e. where it began
● a resource e.g. a raw material or supply of energy
● some information or idea e.g. fieldwork or secondary sources.

---

spatial: refers to changes across the Earth's surface. Geographers look at differences and similarities between one area of space on the surface and others. The study of distributions and patterns across the Earth's surface is a spatial one.

---

specialisation: the concentration of areas and *factors of production* on the job in which they are most productive. For example:
● people specialise on one particular job of work
● land is specialised in its use – either housing, farming, etc.
● countries specialise on particular types of industry e.g. financial services in Switzerland; banana growing in the West Indies.
Specialisation means exchange and trade, and gives rise to greater overall output of goods and services.

---

sphere of influence: the area surrounding a feature such as a settlement, airport or out-of-town shopping centre which:
● is served by and dependent upon the feature, and
● influences the feature.
The sphere of influence of a town will depend upon:
● its size, importance and number of functions/services provided
● the competition from surrounding towns
● transport facilities.
(See *hinterland*.)

---

spillway: a *channel* cut by water escaping from a lake trapped between a glacier and nearby high ground. The lake is called a proglacial lake and contains water from the melting glacier. Newtondale near Pickering is a spillway with steep sides and a flat floor cut by *meltwater* during the last glacial period.

spit: a tongue-shaped *ridge* or embankment of sand and/or shingle projecting into the sea but joined to the land at the other end. Spits:
- are formed by *longshore drift* where *coastlines* change direction, perhaps at a bay or at the mouth of a river
- grow in the direction of the longshore drift
- may have a curved seaward end due to the action of waves from a different direction.

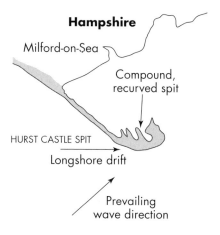

spot height: an accurately surveyed height above sea level. Such heights are:
- often located on roads or hill tops
- marked on Ordnance Survey maps as a numbered dot.

spring-line: a series of points where water emerges at the Earth's surface from underground. Villages are often located at these points. Springs often occur:
- where *permeable* rock (e.g. *chalk*) meets *impermeable* rock (e.g. clay) below
- at the foot of a *scarp*
- at the top of the *water table*.
(See *escarpment*.)

squatter: a person occupying land or property which they neither own nor have any legal rights to. Squatter settlements or *shanty towns* are common in and around *less economically developed country* (LEDC) cities.

stability: the natural tendency of air to remain in position i.e. not to rise; stable air either does not move up or if forced upwards returns to its original position. Rising air is unstable. Whether air is stable or unstable depends on its temperature in relation to that of the surrounding air. Air cooler than that of its surroundings does not rise; it is stable.

stack: a pillar of rock at the seaward end of a *headland*. A stack:
- stands up from the sea bed
- is the result of continued erosion and collapse of the headland by waves
- is a final feature left as the headland erodes
- is eventually worn away itself.

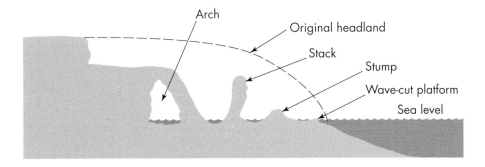

stalactite/stalagmite: columns of pure *limestone* found in caves. Stalactites hang from the roof, and stalagmites form on the floor. Both form from water drips depositing dissolved calcium carbonate. They can join up to form a continuous column as one grows downwards and the other upwards. (See *kant.*)

standard of living: an economist's measure of how well people live. The average level of income per person taken from the *gross national product* (GNP) or *gross domestic product* (GDP) per person is used as this measure. *More economically developed countries* (MEDCs) have higher standards of living than *less economically developed countries* (LEDCs). Their greater wealth means that most people have a lot more money to spend on goods such as food, cars, televisions as well as services such as health care and education. An improved *quality of life* can come from increases in the standard of living.

starvation: death from lack of food, possibly from a general shortage or famine. *Famine* and starvation have become regular occurrences in the *Sahel* countries of Africa during the past 20–30 years.

Stevenson screen: a white, louvred wooden box on legs used for housing meteorological instruments, especially thermometers. The screen:
- shades thermometers from direct sunlight
- allows air to flow freely around the thermometers

so that air or standard temperature can be measured. It is important to measure temperature in a set of standardised conditions so the accurate comparisons between places and at different times can be made.

strip farming: the dividing up of a field into strips of land which are either:
- planted with different crops or
- grazed by animals at different times.

It is an effective way of conserving the soil, especially on sloping ground. Not all the land is bare and vulnerable to *soil erosion* at the same time. Animals graze on one strip at a time, and crop harvesting comes at different times for the various strips.

stump: a short, collapsed *stack*. It represents the very final stage in the *erosion* of a *headland*, starting with a *cave* and progressing to an *arch* and stack.

subduction: an area of the Earth's crust where one tectonic plate descends below another. These areas of subduction:
- occur at *destructive plate boundaries* (see diagram) where plates collide
- generally form *ocean trenches*
- are associated with island arcs or regions of volcanic activity.

A major subduction zone can be found close to the Pacific coast of South America where the Nasca and American Plates collide.

submergence: the *flooding* of coastal areas because of:
- a rise in sea level or
- the sinking of the land.

Former dry land becomes submerged beneath the sea when *estuaries, rias* and *fjords* are formed. Parts of South-East England are at present being gradually submerged. The northern and western parts of Britain covered by glaciers and *ice sheets* during the *Ice Age* are still recovering from that great weight on them by rising, and as they do are slowly tipping the South-East downwards. This was a factor behind the building of the Thames Barrage.

subsidy: a grant of money to support an economic activity. Without this support the activity may not take place. The *European Union*'s *Common Agricultural Policy* (CAP) supports farmers by paying them a subsidy if they export certain products. Paying subsidies is one of the ways in which food supplies can be guaranteed. Subsidies can also be used to keep prices low.

subsistence farming: a farming system in which only enough food to feed the farmer and immediate family is produced. There is virtually none left for sale. It is more common in *less economically developed countries* (LEDCs) than *more economically developed countries* (MEDCs). Lack of capital and machinery is a feature of this system of farming.

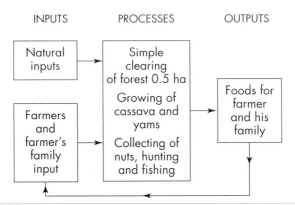

substitution: finding an alternative, perhaps because supplies of an item are running low. A *renewable* source of energy such as *solar* or *wind power* may be a suitable substitute for non-renewable sources such as coal and oil. Substitutes might also be sought where a resource needs conserving for environmental reasons e.g. tropical hardwoods. Recycling of hardwood from, for example, old furniture and developing synthetic materials as a substitute for wood will slow down the rate of deforestation in the tropics.

suburb: the outlying districts of a town/city. These districts close to the edge of the town/city are:
- mainly residential, usually with a low housing density per hectare
- grow outwards and extend the *urban-rural fringe*
- increasingly becoming the location for industrial developments e.g. hi-tech industries and superstores.

The growth of outer suburbs which see the town/city sprawling out into the countryside (i.e. *urban sprawl*) can be described as suburbanisation.

succession: a series of changes which take place to a plant community. This might start with the original colonisation of a locality by a few plants through to the establishment of a *climax vegetation* community e.g. a woodland. (See *sere*.)

sunrise/sunset industry: new and growing, and old and declining industries respectively. Sunrise industries are usually based on the latest technology and inventions/innovations e.g. computers, electronics, lasers. The zone of *hi-tech industries* along the M4 corridor has been called 'sunrise strip'.
Sunset industries, on the other hand, are declining and the industries of the past. They are likely to be producing old-fashioned products with out-of-date technology. The traditional *heavy industries* of engineering, chemicals and textiles in cities such as Sheffield and Manchester might fall into this category.

superstore: a large, usually single-storey, shop selling a wide variety of goods, especially food. They encourage one-stop shopping by car, and often locate by major roads on the edge of towns/cities to take advantage of:
- the space for large car parks
- lower rents
- easy access for car users.

suspension: fine materials such as sand, silt and mud hanging in and carried along by the water of rivers and the sea as it flows. The amount of suspended material in a river increases rapidly as the amount of water in the *channel* increases. Suspension is one of the ways in which water carries its *load* and transports eroded material.

sustainability: this is *development* which combines meeting today's needs with *conser*vation for the future. For example:
- *tropical* rainforests can be managed so that they supply some hardwoods for present needs yet save large areas of healthy, high-quality trees and wildlife
- development projects in *less economically developed countries* (LEDCs) such as power schemes can be designed so that they do not waste resources, use renewable ones where possible and minimise environmental damage yet do improve lives of people today.
Development and environmental management must be long-term and lasting.

swallow (or sink) hole: a vertical or near-vertical shaft, often found in *limestone* areas, through which a surface stream disappears underground. It usually leads to an underground network of *caves* and potholes e.g. Gaping Gill, North Yorkshire. (See *karst*.)

swash: the moving up a beach of a breaking wave. Water and sediment move up the beach. Swash is an important aspect of *constructive waves*, and a key part of the process of *longshore drift*.

syncline: an area of the Earth's crust where the rocks have been *folded* downwards. They form basins e.g. the London Basin.

synoptic chart: a weather map. Symbols are used to show various weather conditions, for example:
- air pressure as isobars
- fronts
- temperature, cloud cover, wind speed and direction and *precipitation* for a series of weather stations in the area of the map.

Synoptic charts for Britain are used to show the weather associated with *depressions* and *anticyclones*.

synthetic: an artificial material. Synthetic materials do not exist in nature and are made by chemical processes e.g. laminates and plastics. Synthetics can be substitutes for natural materials whose supply is beginning to run out e.g. laminated chipboard is used as a substitute for hardwood.

system: a set of related objects. An *ecosystem* is the set of links that exists between *climate*, natural vegetation, animals, soil and rocks. A change in one part of the system affects all others. Systems have *inputs*, processes and *outputs*, each linked together. Farms, firms and river basins can all be studied as systems.

Taiga: the area of coniferous forests close to the Arctic Circle. The short growing season and very cold winters in Scandinavia (Norway, Sweden and Finland), and northern Canada and Russia only allow such hardy trees as fir, pine, spruce and larch to grow.

tariff: an *import* duty. The effect of putting this extra charge on a good which is imported is to increase its price. Governments usually do this in order to cut down on imports. This helps to protect home industries from cheaper foreign competition. The tariffs on cars imported into Japan are very high.

technology park: another name for a *science park* or *business park* where production is of and by high-technology equipment (e.g. lasers, computers). The techniques of production and the products themselves are often both hi-tech. Dundee Technology Park is on a *greenfield site* on the *rural-urban fringe* of Dundee. Sheffield Technology Park has an inner city *brownfield* location. (See *high-tech industry*.)

tectonic activity: the movements of the Earth's crust due to pressures coming from within the Earth. The most extensive type of tectonic activity is the movement of the tectonic plates which make up the Earth's crust. The *folding* and *faulting* of rocks in which they are bent and cracked is tectonic activity. (See *plate tectonics*.)

temperate: the area between the *Tropic* of Cancer and Arctic Circle in the Northern Hemisphere, and between the Tropic of Capricorn and Antarctic Circle in the Southern Hemisphere. In these two mid-*latitude* zones:
- climate tends to be moderate – extremes of temperature and *rainfall* are not found
- grassland and forest occurs.

temperature inversion: when the temperature of the air increases with increased altitude. Normally, temperature decreases with increased altitude. Inversions of temperature are often associated with *anticyclones*. On a clear, calm evening, heavier cool air may roll downhill and collect in a valley bottom.

The air above the valley bottom may be the warmer. This warm layer can trap *pollution*. (See *inversion*.)

temperature profile: a graph plotting temperatures so that it shows variations from either:
- place to place, or
- time to time.

A profile drawn for noon temperatures on 8 February 1999 showed 1°C at Aberdeen, 2°C. at Leeds and Bristol, and 10°C. at Penzance. The profile illustrated below shows the variations during that day at Leeds.

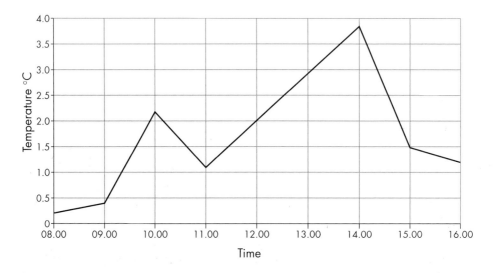

tension: a pulling apart force. Tensional force occurs at:
- *constructive plate boundaries* where the plates move away from each other
- sites of smaller earth movements where faults are the result. Tension cracks the crust and a section of it can subside to leave the other section as a fault.

(See *compression* and *faulting*.)

tenure: the way in which land or property is owned. Three forms of tenure are common in Britain.
- Owned by the occupier.
- Owned by a landlord who receives rent from the occupier.
- Owned by a public authority. This authority too may receive payment for use (e.g. council housing).

terminal moraine: a ridge of material deposited at the front end of a glacier. The deposition occurs at the glacier's most forward position. The deposited material, which includes clay and stones, is known by a variety of names – *boulder clay*, *till* or *ground moraine*. The city of York is partly built on an old terminal moraine.

terracette: a step-like feature, often 20–50 cm in height found on a hill-slope. Terracettes are formed by *soil creep*, and frequently occur as one of a series. (See *soil creep* for diagram.)

terracing: the cutting of flat areas into sloping ground. The flat land is then either farmed or built upon. Many hill-slopes in the Philippines are terraced for wet rice cultivation. The rice is grown in paddy fields on the terraces. Terracing helps to prevent soil *erosion* from a slope by reducing *run-off* and so preventing *gully* formation.

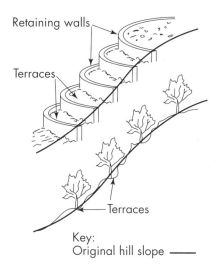

Retaining walls

Terraces

Terraces

Key:
Original hill slope ——

tertiary (tertiarisation): the sector of the economy which includes industries providing services for individuals, the community and other industries, e.g. health, education, transport and retailing. It is generally the largest sector of economic activities in *more economically developed countries* (MEDCs) and often employs more than 50% of the workforce. In *less economically developed countries* (LEDCs) it is generally smaller but usually growing in size.

thermal energy: electricity made by steam powering the generator. The steam comes either from:
● boiling water heated by burning *fossil fuels* such as coal, oil and natural gas, or

- hot water pumped from natural sources underground (i.e. *geothermal energy*).

threshold population: the minimum size of population below which it will not be viable for a place to supply a good or service. Threshold sizes for goods and services depend upon:
- their frequency of use e.g. goods used everyday such as bread require a lower threshold population
- the distance people will travel to buy or use it e.g. greater car ownership has increased the range (the travel distance) of most goods and services.

Some approximate threshold populations in Britain are:

Public house	300
Chemist	4,000
Secondary school	10,000

Fewer people are needed to support a public house to make it profitable than to support a chemist.

throughflow: the flow of water downslope through the soil. This is not the same process as *infiltration*, where the water percolates down rather than through the soil. Throughflow accounts for the movement of some of the water from the land to the sea/oceans. It is strongest where:
- *impermeable* rock prevents infiltration
- there is too much *rainfall* to infiltrate quickly.

(See *hydrological (water) cycle.*)

thunderstorm: the local stormy weather associated with certain cumulonimbus *clouds*. Its weather features include:
- thunder – the noise created when air is heated by lightning, expands rapidly, and then cools and contracts rapidly – thunder can usually be heard up to ten miles away
- lightning – the flash of light or strong electric arc between negatively charged areas in the cloud and positively charged ones on the ground or in another part of the cloud
- heavy *rainfall* and/or hail.

Thunderstorms require heat and moisture to develop, and so are more frequent in:
- summer and inland in Britain
- in warmer locations e.g. Florida.

They are caused by powerful up-currents of air which can lead to the cumulonimbus cloud developing a great height and thickness.

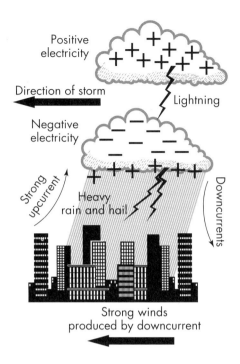

Positive electricity

Direction of storm

Lightning

Negative electricity

Strong upcurrent

Heavy rain and hail

Downcurrents

Strong winds produced by downcurrent

tidal energy: electricity generated by using the tidal rise and fall of the sea. It is a renewable source of energy, which is best generated where the tidal range – the difference between high and low tide – is large. Building *barrages* across *estuaries* with a large tidal range is expensive and can be environmentally damaging. A tidal power station was opened on the estuary of the river Rance near St Malo, Brittany, France in 1966.

tiger economies: the East Asian countries that have experienced very rapid economic development over the past 20–30 years. South Korea, Hong Kong, Taiwan and Singapore are four Tiger economics. They:
- are *newly industrialising countries* (NICs)
- have had great success at exporting their industrial products
- have had the largest *gross national product* (GNP) per person growth rates in the world since the 1960's
- are mainly responsible for the *global shift* in industrial production from the West to the East.

till: a mixture of clay and stones (gravel or small boulders) deposited by ice. It is unsorted and also known as *boulder clay*. It can be smeared over the landscape as a layer or be deposited as distinctive landforms e.g. a *drumlin*.

time zone: a section of the Earth having the same time. Each time zone is 15 degrees of longitude wide, and everywhere in it has a time one hour different to that of is neighbouring time zones. This system reduces the confusion that would exist in all countries if every place used its own sun time. The whole of Britain is in one time zone. It is necessary for the USA to have five time zones; New York is three hours ahead of California and four hours ahead of Alaska.

tombolo: a *spit* connecting an island to the mainland. Chesil Beach has grown in a south-easterly direction from the Dorset coast, eventually joining the Isle of Portland at the other end.

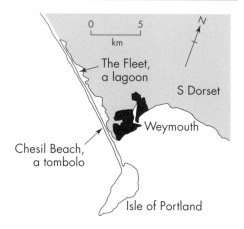

topography: the shape and make-up of the landscape. It includes both:
- natural features e.g. mountains and valleys, and
- artificial features e.g. settlements and roads.

An Ordnance Survey map is a topographical map showing these features to scale.

topological map: a map designed to show only a certain feature e.g. stations on the inter-city rail network of Britain. Locations (e.g. the stations) are shown as dots with the links connecting them as straight lines. Scale and actual shapes are not important. Topological maps are generally used to show all kinds of network.

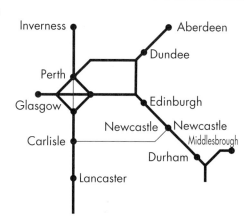

tor: an isolated pile of rounded blocks of rock on a hill-top or *ridge*. It is the remains of the *weathering* of jointed rocks, usually granite or millstone grit. Tors can be found on the granite of Dartmoor and the millstone grit of the Pennines. (See *joint*.)

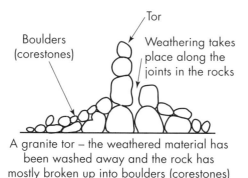

A granite tor – the weathered material has been washed away and the rock has mostly broken up into boulders (corestones)

tornado: a small but very violent revolving storm. Tornados are narrow but tall and contain very strong winds. They occur most frequently in central USA where they are known as twisters. The high heat of these continental areas in summer are responsible for their formation.

tourism: a visit involving at least one overnight stay away from someone's usual home. A holiday is an example of tourism. Tourism can take place:
- in urban and rural areas
- abroad or within the home country.

Tourism has both positive and negative effects on the area visited. The positive effects include:
- job opportunities
- income for economic development.

The negative effects include:
- damage to the environment
- traffic congestion
- dissatisfaction among local people when they compare their own living standards to the much higher living standards of tourists.

town: a settlement intermediate in size and status; its range of functions falls between that of a village and that of a city. The population size of a town can vary between around 4000 (e.g. Bakewell, Derbyshire) and around 90,000 (e.g. Chesterfield, Derbyshire). Towns have a *land use* structure and medium as well as *low-order* functions. One of its *functions* can dominate a town e.g. Chesterfield is an industrial and former mining town.

toxic waste: a source of *pollution* resulting from the use of metals. Metals such as lead, zinc and mercury either give off dangerous fumes or leave behind poisons. These can pollute the air, contaminate the soil and food supplies, and pollute the seas and contaminate fish stocks. The introduction of unleaded petrol is an attempt to reduce the amount of toxic material in the air.

trade: the exchange of goods and services within or between countries. People, regions and countries specialise in certain types of production, and then exchange some or all of these for other goods and services they need. Trade involves goods and services flowing from one place or one set of people where they are made to another place or another set of people where they are bought. When this flow is within one country it is called domestic trade, and when it is across national boundaries (i.e. *imports* and *exports*) it is called international trade.

trade winds: the easterly winds that blow in both hemispheres from the *Tropic* towards the Equator. These winds are the surface air movement part of the Hadley Cell.

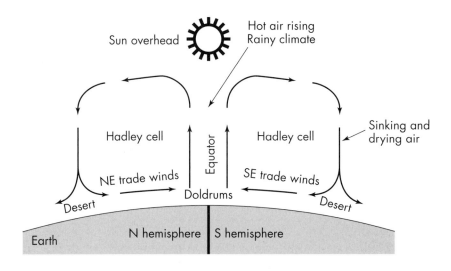

trading bloc: a group of countries organised together for trade. Trade is valuable to a country. Within a trading bloc such as the *European Union* tariffs and customs duties on *imports* would be lowered or abolished altogether. Member countries generally benefit from the extra trade within the group. (See *tariffs*.)

transect: a line which cuts across an area. In fieldwork a transect line can be taken as a means of sampling an area to save studying the whole area. A cross-section can then be drawn along the transect line. A coursework investigation of the different *land uses* within an inner city area might take a say, half-mile transect through this area. Land use types could be plotted along this route and differences noted and explained.

transfer of technology: the movement of ideas and innovations from region to region or from country to country. For example:
- from *more economically developed countries* (MEDCs) to *less economically developed countries* (LEDCs) (e.g. hi-tech farming equipment)
- from one *more economically developed country* (MEDC) to another through a *multi-national company* (e.g. Japanese management styles brought to the *European Union* (EU) countries).

transhumance: the seasonal movement of farmers and their livestock between different pastures in different climates, for instance:
- in Norway and Alpine countries such Switzerland between upland summer pastures and winter valley-bottom pastures
- in *Mediterranean* countries such as Greece between lowland winter pastures and mountain summer pastures.

transition zone: an area on the edge of the inner city surrounding the *central business district* (CBD). It is an area of change, for instance:
- low-cost housing being redeveloped because it is close to facilities of the city centre
- hotels being built on derelict land or where old warehouses were, so pushing the boundary of the CBD outwards.

tramway: a system of rails, largely on public roads, on which tramcars or trams run. In recent years tramways have been re-introduced to some British cities e.g. Sheffield and Manchester. (See *rapid transit system*.)

transmigration: the re-settlement of people within a country according to a government plan. It usually involves *migration* from core regions to periphery regions. The Indonesian Government has been encouraging such migration for some years now. The plan has been for some people to migrate from the over-populated island of Java to less densely populated outer islands such as Sumatra. Deforestation in these outer islands has been a consequence of this transmigration. (See *core and periphery*.)

transnational corporation/company (TNC): a large international company operating across national boundaries, usually in many countries. Hence,
they are named trans- or multi-nationals. Their head offices are normally
located in North America, western Europe or Japan. For example:

- 372 of the 400 largest transnationals have their head offices in these three
  regions
- Unilever, the eighth largest transnational has its head office in London
  and plants in 93 countries.

Key business decisions are made at head office, and these are not necessarily
made in the best interest of the countries where many of the plants are
located. The growth of transnationals has rapid over the past 30–40 years.
The larger transnationals are very powerful economically, and may have
business turnovers greater than the *gross national product* (GNP) of the *less
economically developed countries* (LEDCs) in which they have located.

transpiration: the process in which *water vapour* is given off to the atmosphere from the leaves of plants. It is an important part of *evapotranspiration*
and, as such, of the *water (hydrological) cycle*. Transpiration is strongest in
the most vegetated areas such as forests.

transport network: a pattern in which places (e.g. settlements, stops) are
linked by routes used by a mode of transport (e.g. road, rail). These *networks*
are generally shown as *topological maps*. The development of a transport
network very much reflects the economic development of the country or
region in which it is located (e.g. *more economically developed countries*
(MEDCs) usually have more elaborate and better connected networks than
less economically developed countries (LEDCs)).

tree line: the height above which, or *latitude* beyond which, trees will not
grow. In Britain the tree line is generally reached at about 600 metres above
sea level though in certain locations it is below this. Trees also cannot survive
at high latitudes. This can be seen where the coniferous trees of the *taiga*
give way to the *tundra* areas to the north.

trellised drainage: a rectangular-shaped pattern of river and stream
channels. Channels join the main channel at right angles. This drainage
pattern develops in areas where there are alternating bands of harder and
softer rocks.

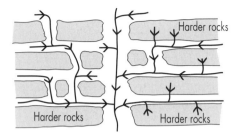

tremor: the shock wave or vibration which shakes the Earth's surface during an *earthquake*. (See *epicentre* and *focus*.)

trend: a general direction of movement. Trends describe the overall picture or general pattern of change rather than individual details. A trend or best-fit line on a *scattergraph* may go through very few actual dots on the graph, but would focus on picking out the general direction of change shown by the dots.

triangular graph: a three-sided graph in the shape of a pyramid on which three sets of data can be plotted. They are commonly used to show information about employment in different types of industry in selected countries. (See *employment structure*.)

tributary: a stream or river which flows into another, usually larger, stream or river. Some rivers have very many tributaries which form part of the river's *drainage basin* (e.g. the river Amazon); other rivers have few tributaries (e.g. the river Nile).

trickle down: the outward spread of the benefits of economic development from the core region where the development was greatest. Wealth can spread throughout periphery regions after development has taken place in a core region. Brazilian Governments have encouraged the growth of a core region, South East Brazil, assuming that the wealth and development will eventually trickle down to other peripheral regions within Brazil. (See *core* and *periphery*.)

tropic: one of the two lines of latitude at 23.5 degrees. The northern tropic is known as the Tropic of Cancer, and that in the Southern Hemisphere as the Tropic of Capricorn. The term tropical describes those parts of the world between the two tropics. Directly overhead sun only occurs in tropical latitudes.

tropical air mass: a stream of hot air originating from a tropical location. There are two main types.

- Tropical continental *air mass* – hot, dry air originating from a tropical continent (e.g. in the Sahara Desert, North Africa)
- Tropical maritime air mass – hot, moist air originating from a tropical ocean (e.g. around the Azores, mid-Atlantic).

tropical cyclone: an area of low atmospheric pressure that forms in tropical latitudes. Tropical *cyclones* are severe cyclones, and can become *hurricanes*.

tropical desert: an area within the Tropics unable to support continuous plant cover, usually because of very low *rainfall*. Tropical deserts are also referred to as hot deserts; very high daytime temperatures accompany very little rainfall in some locations close to the two Tropics, i.e. the Great Australian Desert and the Sahara Desert.

tropical grassland: an area within the Tropics, between the equatorial rainforests and the hot deserts, where grasses are the dominant type of natural vegetation. It is otherwise known as the *savanna*, and has:
- distinct dry and rainy seasons, and
- a rich animal life – the safari parks of East Africa are on the savanna.

tropical monsoon: a seasonal wind in and around the Tropics. In summer this wind brings rain from the cooler tropical oceans to the hotter land areas of southern Asia (e.g. India), and northern Australia. (See *monsoon*.)

tropical rainforest: an area of rich, evergreen forest found around the Equator. The vegetation is well adapted to the year-round hot, wet climate in that:
- it is luxuriant because growth is rapid
- it is layered as the most light-loving trees grow very tall
- there is little undergrowth on the dark forest floor
- the taller trees develop buttresses to support them but no branches which would rob them of strength to grow upwards.

These rainforests have been experiencing rapid *deforestation* in recent years. The effects of this environmental loss are a major cause of concern for many people.

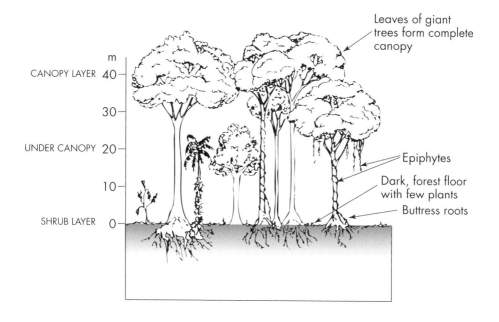

truck farming: the term used in the USA for market gardening. It is the growing of fruit, vegetables and flowers using intensive methods of farming. (See *market gardening*.)

truncated spur: a blunt-ended ridge of rock forming the side of a glaciated valley. A glacier has in the past eroded away the tip of an interlocking spur, leaving it as a truncated one. (See *glacial trough*.)

tsunami: a giant sea wave travelling at high speed. Most tsunamis are caused by underwater *earthquakes*, volcanic eruptions or *landslides*. There may be a series of tsunamis. They slow down and grow higher as they reach the *coastline*, where they can cause great damage and loss of life.

tundra: the barren, periglacial area inside the Arctic Circle (e.g. Siberia, Alaska, northern Canada) where:
- the soil is almost permanently frozen, especially at depth – this is known as *permafrost*
- temperature and rainfall are low – the very harsh winters can last for up to nine months
- there are generally no trees
- vegetation consists of grasses, hardy scrubs, moss and lichen.

The tundra lies to the north of the *taiga* forests.

twilight zone: the run-down, polluted part of the *inner city*. The following are likely to be found:
- decline and decay of old buildings
- derelict land
- low-income, perhaps overcrowded housing
- industrial premises, often old, small and in poor condition
- social problems such as prostitution.

Redevelopment (e.g. renewing houses) will not have taken place as it does in the *transition zone* of the inner city. Twilight zones are often close to the *central business district* (CBD).

typhoon: a violent, revolving tropical storm forming over the China Sea and West Pacific Ocean. It is a *cyclone* which travels westwards towards the coast of eastern Asia (e.g. China, the Philippines) where it can cause large-scale destruction.

underemployment: occurs when the labour force is used wastefully and inefficiently. It usually means that either:
- too many people are doing the work or
- there is not enough work to fully occupy a worker.

In some *less economically developed countries* (LEDCs) there is under employment because there are not enough other resources, especially capital fully to occupy those employed.

undernourishment: a lack of sufficient food over a period of time. It can be measured as a low calorie intake per day, e.g. less than 1500 calories per day. Some people in *less economically developed countries* (LEDCs) are under-nourished and this can lead to:
- diseases being caught, general ill-health and a limited capacity to work
- death by starvation.

underpopulation: occurs when there are too few people in an area to use the other resources (e.g. land) fully. The presence of more people would allow better use of these resources with a resulting general increase in living standards. Canada and Australia are considered to be underpopulated.

uplands: the higher land of an area. It is a relative idea, i.e. high relative to the rest of the area. It would be unusual however to describe an area below about 250 metres in height as an upland.

upward spiral: a process in which an area develops and grows economically. One development leads to another e.g. an industry brings jobs to the area allowing people to spend more in shops creating a demand for more service jobs. A circle or spiral of success is completed when a further twist of the spiral starts. 'Success breeds success' and the 'rich get richer'. (See *cycles of decline or growth*.)

urban climate: the atmospheric conditions experienced in cities and large towns differ from those in the surrounding countryside and are generally:
- warmer
- less sunny

- cloudier, mistier and wetter
- less windy, though in places windier.

The *heat island* effect explains the warmer temperatures of urban climates, and their poorer air quality and higher pollution levels give rise to more *cloud*, *fog*, *mist* and *precipitation*. The effects of urban buildings on wind speeds is shown in the diagram below.

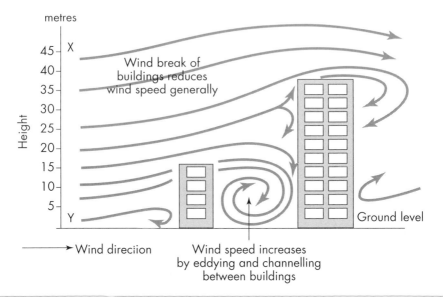

urban decay: the decline and run-down of an area of a city/town, usually an *inner city* area. This run-down can be:
- physical e.g. old, poorly-maintained buildings
- economic e.g. businesses move out of the area so jobs and income are lost
- social e.g. overcrowded houses; vandalism increases.

The *twilight zone* of the inner city experiences urban decay or urban blight as it is also known. Redevelopment is needed. (See *urban redevelopment*.)

Urban Development Corporation (UDC): an agency set up by the British Government to coordinate redevelopment in areas of *urban decay*. Since 1981 there have been UDCs in the run-down city areas of, for example, Merseyside, the London Docklands and Sheffield. They have helped to:
- attract firms to these areas
- renovate and re-use old buildings
- set up environmental improvement schemes.

urban field: another name for a sphere of influence: the area surrounding a settlement that is affected by its activities e.g. the area from which the customers using its functions, such as shops, come from. (See *hinterland*.)

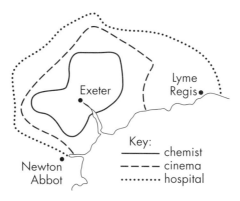

urbanisation: an increase in the percentage of the population living in urban areas (i.e. towns and cities). This can result from:
- rural-to-urban *migration*
- natural population increase in urban areas.

Urbanisation in *more economically developed countries* (MEDCs) accompanied their period of industrialisation in the past. The British population is 89% urbanised. In more recent times urbanisation has become a feature of many *less economically developed countries* (LEDCs).

urban regeneration: the various ways in which an urban area can be improved so that it can again flourish and prosper. These include:
- urban redevelopment i.e. demolishing existing features and replacing them with new structures
- urban renewal i.e. renovating and converting spaces and buildings to new uses.

Inner city areas, including in Britain have been undergoing urban regeneration for the past 30–40 years. Both *redevelopment* (e.g. demolishing steelworks and replacing them with retail outlets in Sheffield) and renewal (e.g. converting a railway station into the G-Mex Centre in Manchester) have been a part of this regeneration. (See *Urban Development Corporation*.)

urban-rural fringe: the area which forms the boundary between the town/city and the countryside. It is usually an area of such features as modern housing, garden centres, new superstores, farms and market gardens. There are likely to be *land use* planning conflicts in this area as the pressures to build on *greenfield sites* around the town/city boundary are strong.

urban sprawl: the outward spread of the urban area of towns and cities into the countryside. The urban-rural fringes tend to change their position over time. Places that were outlying villages in 1915 are now suburbs of Sheffield.

Urban sprawl often takes the form of *ribbon development* as the urban area spreads outwards along main roads.

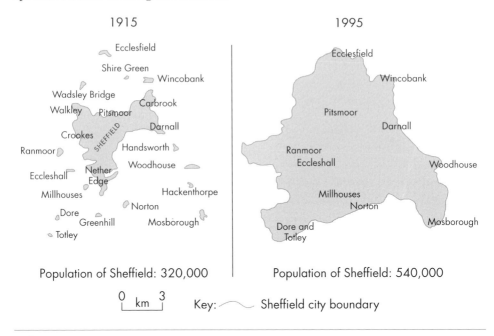

1915

Ecclesfield
Shire Green
Wincobank
Wadsley Bridge
Walkley   Pitsmoor   Carbrook
Crookes   Darnall
SHEFFIELD
Ranmoor   Handsworth
Eccleshall   Nether   Woodhouse
Edge
Millhouses   Hackenthorpe
Dore   Norton
Greenhill   Mosborough
Totley

Population of Sheffield: 320,000

1995

Ecclesfield
Wincobank
Pitsmoor
Darnall
Ranmoor
Eccleshall
Woodhouse
Millhouses
Norton
Dore and
Totley
Mosborough

Population of Sheffield: 540,000

0 km 3   Key: ⌒ Sheffield city boundary

urban structure: the *land use* lay-out of a city/town. It concerns the patterns of land use and the shapes of different land use zones within the city/town.

Urban structure is also known as urban morphology. There are a number of general models of urban land use or morphology, mainly based on ring-shaped zones and/or wedge-shaped zones around the *central business district* (CBD). A model for a typical British city/town is shown below.

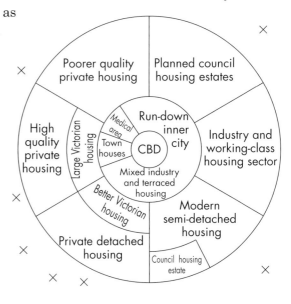

× Dormitory villages – enlarged by 20th century commuter population

u-shaped valley: a *glacial trough* with a U-shaped cross-section. A glacier has flattened the floor and steepened the sides of an existing, probably more V-shaped river valley. *Truncated spurs*, *hanging valleys* and *ribbon lakes* can often be found within U-shaped valleys e.g. those around Snowdon, North Wales.

utilities: industries supplying basic services to the public e.g. electricity, gas, telephones, postal services and water supply. They:
- make use of specialised capital equipment
- require very careful organisation
- may be government-owned and have a monopoly (i.e. only supplier) position.

valley: a long depression between stretches of high ground. Valleys are usually occupied by a stream. On an Ordnance Survey map a valley is shown by the 'V' of the *contour* pattern pointing towards the higher land. Valleys fall into one of a number of types:
- *V-shaped valley* – in some parts of a river valley a V-shaped cross-section will develop. Strong downwards *erosion*, especially near the river's source, will produce this shaped cross-section.
- *U-shaped valley* – glaciated valleys usually have this shape of cross-section.
- Dry valley – a valley without a stream or river. Dry valleys are found on areas of *permeable* rock e.g. chalk.

values: the basic beliefs which lead people to form certain attitudes and opinions about geographical issues such as atmospheric *pollution, greenfield site* developments and poverty in *less economically developed countries* (LEDCs). Caring, preserving and sharing are values. People hold different values and attitudes, and geographers are expected to consider these when arriving at decisions about, for example, *land use*.

velocity: the speed of flow of water or movement of an object. River velocity measures the distance travelled by the water in a set time, usually seconds. It increases with:
- distance downstream
- the slope of the river bed.
Rivers flow faster as they near their mouth, and as the gradient of the bed of the *channel* increases.

vicious circle: the process by which declining areas or activities get gradually poorer and poorer; a *downward spiral* or cycle of decline sets in. (See *cycles of growth and decline*.)

village: a rural settlement with:
- a residential *function*
- a limited range of *low-order* services e.g. church, pub, post office, general store

- a population normally between 200 and 3,000.

Some of the more self-contained and distinctive residential areas of large cities may be known as urban villages e.g. Greenwich Village, New York.

virtuous circle: the process by which developing areas or activities continue to grow and get gradually richer and richer: an *upward spiral* or cycle of growth sets in. (See *cycles of decline and growth*.)

viscosity: the ease with which a liquid substance can flow. The more viscous a liquid, the less easily it flows. *Acid lava* is highly viscous. It is sticky, flows slowly and seldom travels far before solidifying.

visibility: how easily something can be seen. In *weather* and *climate* study, it is the distance at which the furthest object on the ground can be seen. *Fog* and *mist* reduce visibility; they are defined in terms of visibility distances.

visible trade: trade in commodities and manufactured goods. Visibles are tangibles which can be touched. These items are traded internationally. Britain usually *imports* more in value than it *exports*; this gives the country a *balance of trade* deficit. The balance of trade is only concerned with visible trade. (See *invisible trade*.)

volcano: a cone-shaped mountain formed by material ejected from the Earth's interior. Materials such as *lava* and ash pass through a central vent to build the cone around it. Volcanoes can:
- be made of all lava, all ash or layers of both.
- have sides that are either gentle, steep, symmetrical or asymmetrical.
- be active (erupting), extinct (dead) or dormant (quiet but not dead)
- experience violent or steady eruptions.

(See *acid lava*, *basic lava* and *composite volcano*.)

Von Thunen Model: a theory as to how transport and closeness to the food market affects what farmers actually produce. It predicts that:
- bulky, perishable items like vegetables and milk will be produced close to cities/large towns and their market for food, and that
- less bulky, less perishable but more valuable items like cereals and meat will be produced further away from the market.

The model fits many major cities, including London, where vegetables and milk are produced in the immediate surroundings. (See *concentric models*.)

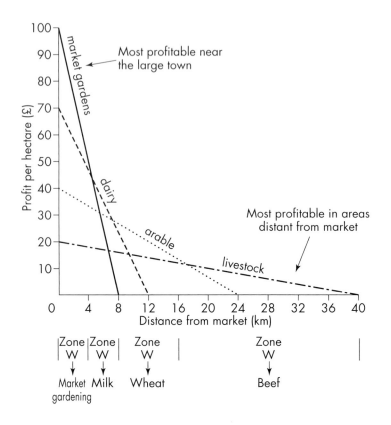

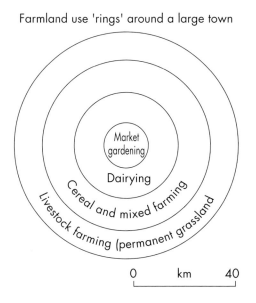

Farmland use 'rings' around a large town

v-shaped valley: a river valley whose cross-section resembles a 'V' in shape. (See *valley*.)

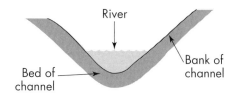

vulcanicity: the ways in which materials from the interior of the Earth affect the surface. These materials are mainly molten *magma* or *lava* but do include ash and cinders. Molten magma will solidify to form *igneous* rock in two locations.

- On the Earth's surface. This is referred to as *extrusive vulcanicity*, and affects surface features directly.
- Within the Earth's crust. This is referred to as *intrusive vulcanicity*, and affects surface features indirectly.

warehousing: the temporary storage of goods by:
- producers, before selling on to their customers
- wholesalers, whose business is to act as 'middlepeople' linking producers and retailers by buying from the former and selling to the latter
- retailers who sell, for example, from shops directly to the public
- owners who do not need to use a good(s) at the present (e.g. furniture).

---

warm front: the boundary in the atmosphere where a warm *air mass* is advancing and replacing colder air. It is called a warm *front* because the temperature at a place rises as the front passes overhead. Warm fronts occur within *depressions*. They bring cloud and rain, often a long period of steady rain.

---

warm sector: the warm air at the centre of a *depression*. The overhead passage of this warm *air mass* part of the depression would be expected to bring:
- rise in temperature
- thinning of the clouds
- the end of any rain.

---

waste disposal: the disposal of solids or liquids not needed by households, industry and public authorities. This involves:
- collection (e.g. domestic refuse collection by lorry; deposit in recycling bins)
- treatment and release into the environment (e.g. sewage treatment plants; *landfill* sites; incinerators).

Environmental damage from the release of too much waste material and from the release of toxic waste into the environment.

---

water balance: the relationship between the input of water to the Earth's surface (e.g. amount of *precipitation*) and the output of water from it (e.g. amount of *evapotranspiration*). This comparison between the input of water and the output of water can be done at various *scales* e.g. continental scale for the whole area of a continent or at drainage basin scale for the area drained by one river. A positive water balance, i.e. input of precipitation exceeds output of evapotranspiration, *run-off* and the creation of a drainage network of rivers and streams. Deserts have a water balance deficit, i.e. output equals all inputs, present and past.

water cycle: the movement of water in liquid and vapour form through various environments, i.e. the atmosphere, sea, land surface and underground. (See *hydrological cycle* and *water vapour*.)

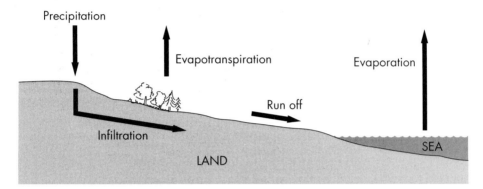

waterfall: a vertical 'wall' of water along the course of a stream or river. It occurs where the stream or river flows over a band of hard rock. The softer rock downstream of the hard band becomes eroded away leaving a vertical drop down which the water falls. Waterfalls usually retreat upstream as *erosion* of the hard band occurs.

High Force Waterfall, North Yorkshire.

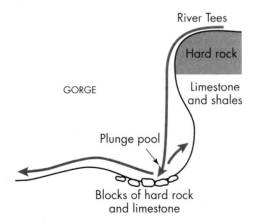

waterlogged: describes a soil saturated with water. Waterlogging occurs below the *water table*. During periods of *flooding* when the water table is above the surface all the soil is waterlogged. (See *saturation*.)

watershed: the boundary between two *drainage basins*. It is usually a ridge of high ground. This divide between drainage basins does shift in time.

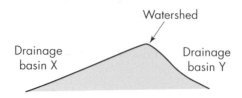

water supply: the availability of water for human use. The main sources of water supply are:
- reservoirs
- rivers
- wells and boreholes
- treated sea water (i.e. desalination).

Supplying areas of high water demand (e.g. large cities) usually means transferring it from one place to another, e.g. water collected in Central Wales is transferred by pipeline to Birmingham.

water table: the top of the *aquifer* or the water level, normally underground. This level is usually below ground, and rises or falls according to:
- the relief of the land surface above it
- weather conditions e.g. the water table falls during a drought but rises during heavy rain.

Where the water table is exposed springs can occur.

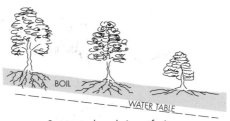

Saturated rock (aquifer)

water vapour: water in a gaseous rather than liquid form. Water in its liquid form becomes vapour through evaporation into the air; *condensation* will return water vapour to its liquid form (e.g. rainfall).

wave: a ridge of water formed by the wind. Waves help to shape the *coastline* by *erosion* and *deposition*. *Constructive waves* are more depositional than erosional because their *swash* is stronger than their *backwash*. *Destructive waves* have a stronger backwash than swash and therefore cause more erosion than deposition.

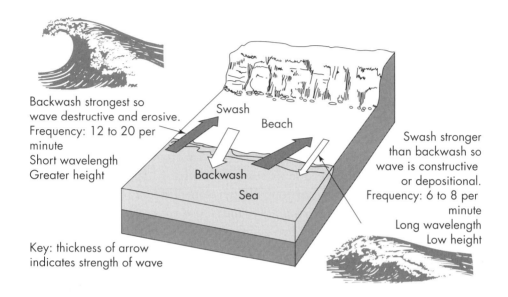

Backwash strongest so wave destructive and erosive.
Frequency: 12 to 20 per minute
Short wavelength
Greater height

Swash

Beach

Backwash

Sea

Swash stronger than backwash so wave is constructive or depositional.
Frequency: 6 to 8 per minute
Long wavelength
Low height

Key: thickness of arrow indicates strength of wave

wave-cut platform: a level or gently sloping rock surface along a shoreline, often at the foot of cliffs. It is an erosional feature which has been cut by wave action as the cliffs are eroded and retreat inland. Wave-cut platforms are often covered by the sea at high tide and exposed at low tide. (See *stack* for diagram.)

wave power: electricity generated by the energy of the waves. This is a possible alternative source of power to nuclear and burning fossil fuels, but it has generally not yet been developed sufficiently to make it a commercial success. One device that has been developed is a floating boom which drives a generator by bobbing up and down with the waves. (See *alternative energy*.)

wave refraction: the bending of waves as they reach the shoreline. The shallower water near the coast causes this bending to occur. It is an important process along *coastlines* of *headlands* and *bays*. The refraction of the waves along these coastlines can cause them to break directly on the side of the headland. This concentrates the erosional power of the waves and leads to the formation of *caves* and natural *arches*.

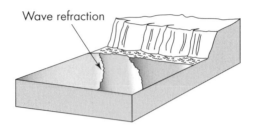

Wave refraction

wealth: how well off people, regions or countries are in a financial sense. Wealth can be held in cash, company shares, property or material possessions. *Gross domestic or national product* (GDP/GNP) are usually taken as the main single measure of the wealth of a country. High GDP/GNP per person countries are normally referred to as *more economically developed countries* (MEDCs). The phrase 'more economically developed' refers to their generally higher level of wealth. *Less economically developed countries* (LEDCs) have lower GDP/GNPs per person and so generally lower levels of wealth.

weather: the condition of the *atmosphere* at any moment of time. This condition results from the state of a number of elements, each of which can be measured and recorded, for instance:
- air temperature measured in °C using a maximum-minimum thermometer
- rainfall measured in millimetres using a raingauge
- wind speed measured in knots using an anemometer.

The essence of weather, especially in Britain is change. It can change by the hour, and from day to day. Any period of time during which the weather conditions remain constant is known as a weather window; the length of the window can be measured. Weather recordings are averaged to give *climate* figures.

weathering: the breakdown of rock on the spot through exposure to the environment, especially the *weather*. The various weathering factors can be classified into three groups.
- A *mechanical weathering* group e.g. *freeze-thaw* where water in rock joints freezes, expands and shatters the rock.
- A *chemical weathering* group e.g. the solution of *limestone* in rainwater.
- A *biological weathering* group e.g. tree roots embedding themselves in rock and causing it to break up; acids from decaying plants and dead organisms such as worms help rocks to disintegrate.

The three groups usually occur together but one may be stronger than the others depending on the *climate*, e.g. in tropical climates the high temperatures and heavy rainfall encourage chemical weathering. This weathering is not the same as erosion because there is no movement or transport of the broken-down material.

weather plot: the collection of *weather* symbols shown on a weather map for a particular weather station e.g. Leeds weather station on a *synoptic chart* for Britain. They are based on the standard weather map symbols.

welfare: the well-being of people in the widest sense. The quality of human life is more than a financial matter. Attempts to measure differences in *quality of life* between people and places examine the extent to which basic human needs and rights are met, for instance:
- social needs such as the right to personal safety and security – crime rates help here
- educational needs such as the right to read and write (i.e. the adult *literacy rate*)
- health needs such as the right to survive the first year of life (i.e. the *infant mortality rate*).

(See *human welfare*.)

well: a hole dug into the ground with water at the bottom. Wells are dug so as to obtain underground supplies of water, and need to penetrate the *aquifer* well below the *water table*. The water can then:
- be pumped to the surface
- be lifted by bucket to the surface
- rise to the surface naturally in the case of an *artesian well*.

Digging wells and installing a pump is a popular development project in the villages of *less economically developed countries* (LEDCs).

westerlies: the prevailing winds that blow from the west in the *temperate* latitudes of both hemispheres. They are the prevailing winds over Britain and bring much of its weather, including *depressions* and *anticyclones*.

West Pacific rim: the Asian countries, most of which are either industrialised (e.g. Japan) or newly industrialised (e.g. Taiwan) with coastlines on the western shore of the Pacific Ocean. The term is usually used in an economic and industrial sense. It is this region which now produces a large proportion of the world's manufactured goods. It is also the western rim of the *Pacific 'Ring of Fire'*. (See *newly industrialising country*.)

wetland: a natural and permanent area of saturated soil and perhaps land with standing water on it. Marsh, fen, bog and *flood plain* are wetland. They are often rich in wildlife and capable of being very fertile agriculturally. Some of the Lincolnshire and Cambridgeshire Fens have been drained for farming. Such developments can threaten the wetland environment.

wetted perimeter: that part of a river or stream's *channel* which is wet because it is in contact with the water in the channel. A cross-section of the channel can be drawn, the wetted area of the bed and banks shown and the total length of this area calculated.

wind action: the effects of the air moving from places of high pressure to places of lower pressure. These effects can be:
- *erosion* of rocks and materials on the surface (e.g. the wind armed with particles can be 'sand-blast' rock surfaces)
- transportation and *deposition* of loose materials (e.g. sand grains carried by the wind can be deposited to form sand dunes)
- the perception that it is colder, when temperatures are low, than it really is – wind-chill is the cooling effect of wind on the skin when temperatures are low.

Many of the landforms along coastlines and in deserts (e.g. sand dunes) show the importance of the wind as an erosional and depositional factor.

wind belt: an area of the Earth's surface where the weather pattern is dominated by a *prevailing wind* e.g. the *trade winds* in the *Tropics*.

wind break: a means of providing shelter from strong or persistent winds. The means available include:
- trees
- walls
- hedges.

These can be either naturally occurring or placed there by people (e.g. by planting a line of trees). They can provide shelter for crops, buildings or soil, and are most commonly found in rural farming areas. There may be a need to prevent damage to farmhouses, buildings and crops, and to prevent soil *erosion*.

wind gap: a pass through an *upland* or *ridge* not occupied by a river. Although the wind blows through this gap, it will not have been formed by the wind but rather cut by running water, for instance:
- by *meltwater* during the *Ice Age*
- by a river which has now been diverted
- by a river which has now dried up.

Wind gaps can be found in the chalk downs of southern England.

wind power: electricity generated from windmills and wind turbines. A large area of such machinery is known as a wind farm (e.g. Delabole, North Cornwall). They do provide some electricity and are one of the alternative sources of energy to nuclear and the burning of fossil fuels. However:

- the wind does not blow constantly, creating problems of an unreliable supply
- some people object to the appearance and noise of modern windmills and turbines.

(See *alternative energy*.)

wind rose: a diagram which shows the number of days that the wind has blown from each direction in one year at a weather station. The length of the line at each of the major compass points indicates the frequency of the wind from that direction.

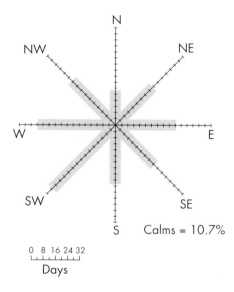

wind vane: an instrument used to show wind direction. It is essentially a horizontal arm or finger which lines up with the wind. One end is pushed away from the direction from which the wind is blowing so that the other turns to show the direction of the wind.

windward: the side of a feature (e.g. a building) which faces into the wind.

World Bank: an international bank set up in Washington DC, USA, to provide aid to *less economically developed countries* (LEDCs). Its business is the development of these countries by:

- providing loans for projects to improve the country's *infrastructure* e.g. road building
- offering technical assistance and advice
- helping with difficulties with foreign trade and debts.

xerophyte: a plant adapted to living in dry conditions e.g. *deserts*. Cacti and palm trees are *drought*-resistant and xerophytic. They survive in these conditions for various reasons, for instance:

- they may have long roots enable them to reach underground water supplies
- they may have fleshy stems in which to store water
- they may have thick bark or waxy leaves to reduce *transpiration*.

Xerophytic plants are likely to be at a stage in a plant *succession*. A plant succession that develops in these very dry conditions is referred to as a xerosere. (See *sere*.)

yield: the outcome or end product of an activity. In agriculture, yield usually refers to the *output* (e.g. crops, milk) expressed in terms of an *input*, for instance:

- wheat yield per hectare
- milk yield per cow
- grape yield per person.

Therefore it becomes a way of measuring agricultural productivity. Yields per unit of area are higher in *intensive farming* than *extensive farming*. With the intensification of farming in recent times, especially in *more economically developed countries* (MEDCs), yields per unit of area have risen considerably.

youthful population: a population with a young average age and a high proportion of children and young people in it. The high birth rate in some *less economically developed countries* (LEDCs) gives them an increasing number of young people and a youthful population structure. This creates an unfavourable *dependency ratio* for the country with large numbers of young non-workers depending upon the support of those in work.

Z

zero growth: refers to a population which is neither increasing nor decreasing in overall size. Births merely replace deaths. The *birth rate* and the *death rate* are the same. This is approximately the position in Britain and much of the rest of the *European Union* at present.

zonal soil: a type of soil formed under the strong influence of *climate* and vegetation in one of the standard climatic and vegetational regions of the world. Zonal soils are mature soils with distinctive *profiles* and clear *horizons*. They can be mapped in belts on a world map, for example:
- *chernozems* on the grasslands of the North American prairies and Russian steppes with their distinctive climate
- *podsols* in the *taiga* forests of Scandinavia, Canada and Russia.

CLASSIFICATION AND USE OF TERMS

In this section you will find the various terms defined and explained in this book classified under the headings of the main topics and themes in geography. At the end of each headed list of terms are examples of two shorter GCSE questions in which some of these terms are used. Acceptable answers are given on page 221.

I Agriculture

Agribusiness
Agricultural revolution (new)
Arable
Battery farming
Cash crops
Collective farming
Commercial farming
Common Agricultural Policy (CAP)
Concentric models
Contour ploughing
Contract farming
Co-operative farming
Dairy farming
Extensive farming
Factory farming
Fertiliser
Fertility
Fodder crop
Food surplus
Green revolution
Growing season
High-yielding variety (HYV)
Hill farming
Horticulture
Input
Intake
Intensive
Intermittent cropping
Irrigation
Land consolidation

Land reform
Land use
Land value
Market gardening
Mixed farming
Monoculture
Nomadic pastoralism (herding)
Organic farming
Output
Overgrazing
Overproduction
Pastoral
Plantation
Prairie
Primary sector/industry
Quota
Ranching
Rotation
Rough grazing
Sedentary
Self-sufficiency
Set-aside
Shifting cultivation
Strip farming
Subsistence farming
Terracing
Transhumance
Truck farming
Von Thunen model
Yield

GCSE example question: 1 Agriculture

The map below shows some of the main types of farming found in the world.

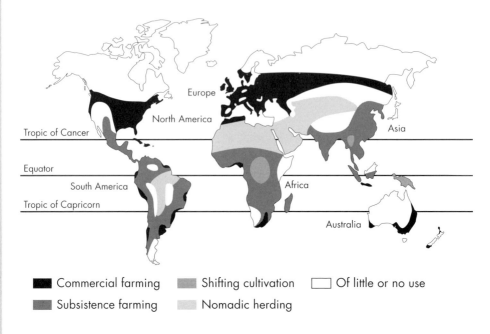

Commercial farming Shifting cultivation Of little or no use
Subsistence farming Nomadic herding

a) Name:
   (i)   the main type of farming in Europe
   (ii) two types of farming found in Africa
   (iii) a continent in which shifting cultivation is found.
b) Below are four definitions, one for each of the following four types of
    farming – commercial farming; shifting cultivation, subsistence farming;
    nomadic farming – but not in that order. Name the type of farming
    defined in each of the cases.
   (i)   People grow enough food to live on but have little to sell.
   (ii) People wander from place to place living on milk and meat from their
         cattle, sheep or camels.
   (iii) Crops are grown in a small forest clearing for a short period of time
         before the farmer moves on to another clearing.
   (iv) Animals and crops are produced for sale, often using modern
         machines and methods.
c) Certain types of farming are typical of areas of the world with differing
    levels of economic development.
   (i)   The diagram below shows average income per person – a measure of
         economic development in an area. Complete the boxes with the
         appropriate type of agriculture using the following list.
         • Commercial farming.

- Subsistence farming.
- Peasant farming. (Some produce consumed by farmer; some sold.)

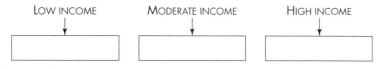

LOW INCOME   MODERATE INCOME   HIGH INCOME

(ii) Explain one of your answers.

2 Atmosphere (weather and climate)

Acid rain
Air mass
Anemometer
Anticyclone
Arid
Aspect
Atmosphere
Barometer
Beaufort Scale
Buys Ballots Law
Climate
Climatic change
Climatic region
Climatograph
Clouds
Cold front
Condensation
Continentality
Convection
Convectional rain
Cyclone
Depression
Dew
Drought
Equatorial climate
Evapotranspiration
Eye
Fog
Front
General circulation
Global warming

Greenhouse effect
Gulf stream
Heat island
Humidity
Hurricane
Hygrometer
Insolation
Instability
Inversion
Jet stream
Lapse rate
Leeward
Low
Maximum-minimum thermometer
Mediterranean
Micro-climate
Mist
Monsoon
Natural hazard
Occlusion
Ocean current
Orographic rain
Ozone layer
Precipitation
Pressure (air)
Radiation
Radiation fog
Rainfall
Rain gauge
Rainshadow
Range

Relative humidity	Tropical cyclone
Relief rainfall	Tropical monsoon
Ridge	Typhoon
Sleet	Urban climate
Smog	Visibility
Snow	Warm front
Stability	Warm sector
Stevenson Screen	Water vapour
Synoptic chart	Weather
Temperate	Weather plot
Temperature inversion	Westerlies
Temperature profile	Wind belt
Thunderstorm	Wind break
Tornado	Wind rose
Trade winds	Wind vane
Tropical air mass	Windward

GCSE example question: 2 Atmosphere

The diagram below shows a cross-section through a weather system.

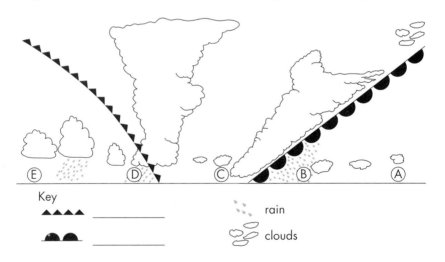

Key

▲▲▲▲ _____   `rain`

●●● _____   `clouds`

(a) What name is given to the weather system shown?

(b) (i) Draw a large arrow on the diagram to show the probable direction in which the weather system is moving.

    (ii) Which symbol means 'warm front' and which means 'cold front' on the diagram's key?

(c) Study the weather conditions below, which occur at three of the points (A, B, C, D and E) on the diagram.

Weather conditions	Letter
Wind changes direction. Pressure is falling and temperature is rising. Continuous rain.	
Temperature is falling and pressure is rising. Occasional showers. Visibility is good.	
Pressure is falling. Cloud cover thickens as warm air rises above the cold air ahead.	

Choose the correct letter for each set of conditions and write it in the appropriate box above.

(d) Which word below best describes the atmospheric pressure in the weather system shown on the diagram? Tick the correct box.

Low ❏   Medium ❏   High ❏

(NEAB)

3 Coasts

Arch
Backwash
Bar
Bay
Beach
Cave
Cliff recession
Coastline
Constructive waves
Delta
Destructive waves
Dune
Dyke
Emergent coast
Fjord
Gabions
Groyne
Headland
Hydraulic action
Lagoon
Land reclamation

Longshore drift
Marine/maritime
Offshore bar
Polder
Raised beach
Reclamation
Refraction
Revetment
Ria
Sea Defences
Sea level
Spit
Stack
Stump
Submergence
Swash
Tombolo
Tsunami
Wave
Wave-cut platform
Wave refraction

GCSE example question: 3 Coasts

Study the sketch below, which shows a coastal headland at low tide.

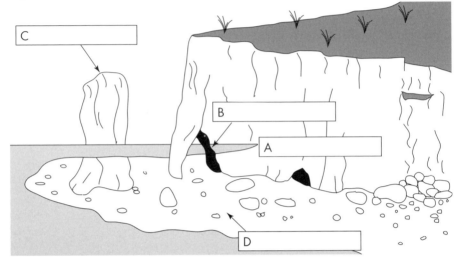

(a)　Name the features shown at A, B, C and D.

(b)　Explain with the aid of diagrams how feature C may have been formed

(SEG)

4 Development and welfare

Absolute poverty

Adult literacy rate

Aid

Appropriate technology

Assisted areas

Backwash

Brandt report

Capital

Conflict of interest

Core and periphery

Cycles of decline or growth

Cycle of poverty (deprivation)

Debt

Deprivation

Development

Development area

Development gap

Downward spiral

Economic development

Employment structure

Enterprise zone

European Union (EU)

Famine

Feedback

Formal sector

Globalisation

Government subsidy

Gross domestic product/gross national product (GDP/GNP) per person

Growth pole

Human welfare

Industrial revolution

Informal sector

Infrastructure

Interdependence

Intermediate technology
Inward investment
Less economically developed country
   (LEDC)
Malnutrition
More economically developed country
   (MEDC)
Multiplier effect
Neo-colonialism
Newly industrialising country (NIC)
Outward investment
Periphery
Private sector
Public sector
Quality of life
Redevelopment
Regional imbalance/policy
Relative poverty
Resource
Rural development

Sector
Self-help scheme
Standard of living
Starvation
Subsidy
Substitution
Sustainability
Tenure
Tiger economies
Transfer of technology
Trickle-down
Underemployment
Undernourished
Upward spiral
Vicious circle
Virtuous circle
Wealth
Welfare
West Pacific Rim
World Bank

GCSE example questions: 4 Development and welfare

(a) The table shows some of the types of aid that are sent from more economically developed countries (MEDCs) to less economically developed countries (LEDCs).

   (i) What is the meaning of the term 'short-term aid'?

   (ii) Name one other example of a type of short-term aid.

Short-term aid	Long-term aid
Food aid, blankets and tents	Education and training
Lorries, medicines	Capital investment
	Transport, improvement schemes

   (iii) State briefly why long-term aid may be of more use to a less economically developed country (LEDC).

(b) Study this newspaper extract.

   (i) What term is used for aid that has conditions linked with it?

   (ii) What are the advantages to Britain of this type of deal?

Aid is given by the government of one country to another. Often the aid must be spent on goods and services from the country providing the aid.

For example, the British Government paid for the building of a major new tarmac road in Kenya, and a British construction firm was awarded the contract.

(ii) State one disadvantage to Kenya of this type of deal.

(SEG)

5 Energy

Alternative energy

Barrage

Biomass

Energy

Fossil fuels

Geothermal energy

Hydro-electric power (HEP)

Mineral extraction

National grid

Natural gas

Natural resource

Non-renewable

Nuclear power

Open-cast mining

Power station

Primary energy

Quarrying

Renewable resource

Solar

Thermal energy

Tidal energy

Wave power

Wind power

GCSE example question: 5 Energy

The table shows some of the natural resources that can be used to generate electricity.

Renewable sources of energy	Non-renewable sources of energy
Wind	Coal
Solar	Peat
Tides	Uranium

(a) What is the meaning of the term 'renewable sources of energy'?

(b) Name one other renewable source of energy, not shown in the table.

(c) State briefly why coal is used to make electricity rather than used directly as a source of energy.

(SEG)

6 Landforms, processes and glaciation

Abrasion	Limestone
Alluvium	Mass movement
Arete	Mechanical weathering
Attrition	Meltwater
Avalanche	Metamorphic
Base level	Moraine
Bedding plane	Periglacial
Biological weathering	Permafrost
Boulder clay	Permeable
Carboniferous limestone	Physical weathering
Cave	Plain
Chalk	Plateau
Chemical weathering	Plucking
Corrasion	Porous
Debris	Pot hole
Deflation	Pyramidal peak
Deposition	Relief
Drumlin	Resistance
Dry valley	Ribbon lake
Dune	Ridge
Erosion	Rift valley
Escarpment	Rock
Exfoliation	Saltation
Freeze-thaw	Scarp
Geomorphic processes	Schist
Glacial trough	Scree
Glaciation	Sedimentary
Glacier	Shield
Gorge	Slate
Hanging valley	Slumping
Hydrolysis	Solution
Ice Age	Spillway
Ice sheet	Stalactite
Igneous	Stalagmite
Impermeable	Swallow/sink hole
Joint	Syncline
Karst	Terminal moraine
Landform	Terracette
Landslide	Till

Tor

Truncated spur

Tundra

Valley

U-shaped valley

Weathering

Wind action

Wind gap

GCSE example question: 6 Landforms, processes and glaciation

Study the sketch map below, showing a highland area that used to be glaciated.

(a) Name the glacial features at A, B, C and D.

(b) Describe and explain the shape of the feature at D.

7 Leisure and services

Areas of outstanding natural beauty

Business park

Employment structure

Footloose

Homeworking

Honeypot

Hypermarket

Invisibles

Market

National Park

Out-of-town location

Post-industrial society

Quaternary

Recreation

Retail park

Service

Shopping mall/centre   Tourism
Superstore   Utilities
Tertiary   Warehousing

GCSE example question: 7 Leisure and services

(a) Industry can be divided into three categories: primary, secondary and tertiary. The table below shows a number of secondary and tertiary industries. Complete the boxes in the grid below with the correct category of industry.

Category	Example
	Chemical works
	Historic ship centre
	Telephone call centre
	Oil refinery

(b) (i) Study the list of jobs in tertiary industry printed below. Indicate by means of a tick (✔) whether they are in the formal or informal sector.

Job	Formal	Informal
Bank clerk in Tokyo		
Shoe shine person in Sao Paulo		
Street car washer in London		
Government official in Los Angeles		
Street food seller in Mexico City		

    (ii) Explain the difference between the formal and informal sectors of the economy.

(c) A superstore is a good example of a tertiary industry. Over the last 20 years, superstores have moved to new sites on the edge of towns. What advantage does this location have for a superstore?

(d) The development of new service industries can take place in old properties and on derelict land, as well as on greenfield sites. Explain why old properties or derelict land are sometimes used in this way.

Classification and use of terms for GCSE

8 Manufacturing industry

Agglomeration	Labour-intensive
Automation	Light industry
Brownfield site	Localisation
Business park	Manufacturing
Capital-intensive	Market
Cottage industry	Mass production
Decentralisation	Material-orientation
Deglomeration	Mechanisation
De-industrialisation	Multi-national corporation/
Diversification	company (MNC)
Economies of scale	Output
Employment structure	Out-of-town location
Extractive industry	Pacific Rim
Factors of production	Raw material
Footloose	Recycling
Global shift	Science Park
Greenfield site	Secondary
Heavy industry	Sunrise/Sunset industry
High-tech. industry	synthetic
Industrial estate	Technology Park
Industrial inertia	Transnational corporation (TNC)
Industrial revolution	Toxic waste
Input	Waste disposal
Integration	

GCSE example question: 8 Manufacturing industry

(a) Choose a manufacturing industry you have studied. Complete this diagram to show the industry as a system.

Chosen industry..

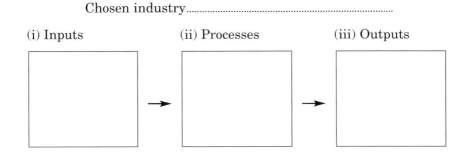

(i) Inputs   (ii) Processes   (iii) Outputs

(b) The diagram below shows what the owner must think about when choosing a location for a new factory. How can government policy affect the location of a factory?

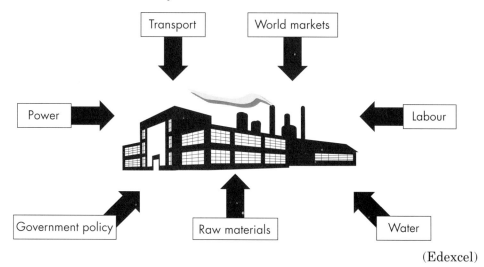

Transport

World markets

Power

Labour

Government policy

Raw materials

Water

(Edexcel)

9 Mapwork and graphicacy

Aerial photographs
Altitude
Annotation
Bar chart
Cartography
Chloropleth
Continent
Contour
Desire line
Distribution
Flow line
Gradient
Graphicacy
Grid reference
Isopleth
Key
Latitude
Location
Longitude
Mental map
National grid

Pie-graph/chart
Region
Relief
Ridge
Satellite image
Scale
Scattergraph
Secondary
Skills
Source
Spatial
Spot height
System
Time zone
Topography
Topological map
Transect
Trend
Triangular graph
Tropic
Uplands

GCSE example question: 9 Mapwork and graphicacy

The following triangular graph and the table below it give information about employment in different types of industry in selected countries.

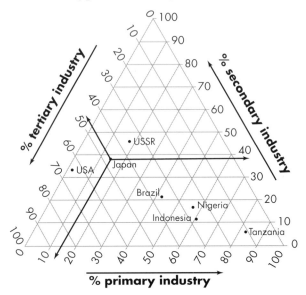

Country	Percentage of workforce employed in:			Level of development (economic)
	primary industry	secondary industry	tertiary industry	
Tanzania	83	6	11	LEDC
Indonesia				
Nigeria	56	17	27	
Brazil	41	22	37	
Jamaica	28	17	55	
USSR	17	47	36	
Japan	13	39	48	
USA	2	33	65	MEDC

(a) (i) Complete the table to show the figures for Indonesia.
    (ii) Complete the triangular graph by plotting the position of Jamaica.

(b) Give an example of an occupation in each of the following types of industry.
    (i) Primary industry.
    (ii) Secondary industry.
    (iii) Tertiary industry.

(c) 'As a country develops economically, its employment structure changes'.
    Use the graph and table to explain this statement.   (Edexcel)

10 Plate tectonics

Acid lava
Basic lava
Composite volcano
Compression
Conservative plate boundary
Constructive plate boundary
Continental plate
Convergent plate boundary
Crater
Crust
Destructive plate boundary
Divergent plate boundary
Dormant
Dyke
Earthquake
Epicentre
Extrusive
Faulting
Folding
Hazard (natural)
Igneous
Intrusive

Lava
Magma
Mantle
Mid-ocean ridge
Ocean trench
Pacific Ring of Fire
Parasitic cone
Tectonic plate
Pyroclast
Richter scale
Rift valley
Seismograph
Shield
Sill
Subduction
Tectonic activity
Tension
Tremor
Viscosity
Volcano
Vulcanicity

GCSE example question: 10 Plate tectonics

Study the diagram. Which of the locations A to E is:

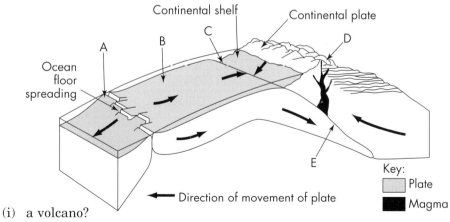

(i)   a volcano?
(ii) an oceanic plate?
(iii) an ocean trench?
(iv) a zone of earthquakes deep under the ground?

11 Population

Ageing population	Optimum population
Birth rate	Out-migration
Census	Overcrowding
Counter-urbanisation	Overpopulation
Death rate	Population distribution
Demographic (population) transition model	Population explosion
	Population pyramid
Density of population (population density)	Population structure
	Positive discrimination
Dependency ratio	Push-and-pull model
Emigration	Refugee
Equal opportunities	Rural depopulation
Fertility	Second home
Guest worker	Segregation
Hostile environment	Socio-economic
Immigration	Squatter
Infant mortality rate	Transmigration
In-migration	Underpopulation
Life expectancy	Urbanisation
Migration	Youthful population
Multi-cultural	Zero growth
Natural increase	

GCSE example question: 11 Population

Some factors affecting population density	
List A Title:	List B Title: ....
1 Vegetation	1 Transport
2 Soils	2 Technology
3 Mineral resources	3 Government investment
4	4 ....

(a) (i) Study the table above. Then select from the titles given below one title for List A and one for List B, and write them in the spaces provided.

Distribution Human Positive Natural Density Negative

(ii) Complete both List A and List B by adding a fourth example of your own, of the type of factors shown in each list.

(iii) What is meant by the term population density?

(b) Select either one densely populated area, or one sparsely populated area.

| Scottish Highlands   Californian coast   Sahara desert   SE England |

(i) Name your chosen area and state whether it is densely populated or sparsely populated.

(ii) Suggest reasons for the population density found in your chosen area.

(NEAB)

12 Running water and drainage

Aquifer	Knickpoint
Artesian well	Lag time
Bankfull	Levee
Base flow	Load
Braiding	Long profile
Catchment area	Meander
Channel	Mouth
Confluence	Multi-purpose
Dendritic	Ox-bow lake
Desalination	Parallel drainage
Discharge	Peak flow
Distributary	Percolation
Drainage basin	Plunge pool
Dyke	Pool
Estuary	Radial drainage
Flooding	Rapids
Flood plain	Rejuvenation
Fluvial	Reservoir
Groundwater	Riffle
Hydraulic action	River capture
Hydrograph	River cliff (bluff)
Water (hydrological) cycle	River management
Infiltration	River terrace
Interception	Run-off
Interlocking spur	Saturation
Intermittent stream	Senuosity

Classification and use of terms for GCSE

Source	Water balance
Suspension	Water cycle
Throughflow	Waterfall
Transpiration	Waterlogged
Trellised drainage	Watershed
Tributary	Water supply
Velocity	Well
V-shaped valley	Wetted perimeter

GCSE example question: 12 Running water and drainage

Rainfall and river depth for a town in a more economically developed country (MEDC)

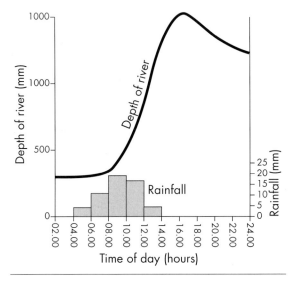

(a) (i) Study the graph above. How long was the time lag?

    (ii) Give two reasons why there was this 'time lag'.

(b) (i) Explain why the shape of a river valley near its source and near its mouth are different.

    (ii) Natural river banks called levees are found in some rivers. Using labelled diagrams, explain how a levee is formed.

(c) The river described by the above chart floods more frequently now than before the main urban area through which it flows was built. Suggest three reasons for this.

(d) For a named example you have studied, explain why the effects of flooding are often greater in a LEDC than in a MEDC.

                                                                    (MEG)

13 Settlement

Bid-rent
Bosnywash
Bridge point
Catchment area
Central business district (CBD)
Commune
Comparison goods
Concentric models
Conurbation
Convenience goods
Dispersed settlement
Dormitory settlement
Ethnic area
Functions
Functional zone
Gentrification
Ghetto
Green belt
Hamlet
Hierarchy
High-order
Hinterland
Inner city
Land use
Land value
Linear
Low-order
Market town
Megalopolis
Million-city
Morphology
Neighbourhood
New Town
Nucleated

Ordinary business district (OBD)
Order of good/service
Overspill
Owner-occupier
Peak land value intersection (PLVI)
Planning
Range
Rank-size rule
Resettlement
Residential type
Resort
Ribbon development
Rural-urban/Urban-rural fringe
Service
Shanty town (spontaneous squatter settlement
Site and situation
Slum
Sphere of influence
Spring-line
Suburb
Threshold population
Town
Transition zone
Twilight zone
Urban decay
Urban Development Corporation (UDC)
Urban field
Urban regeneration
Urban sprawl
Urban structure
Village

GCSE example question: 13 Settlement

Study the diagram above showing land use zones and land values in a city in a MEDC.

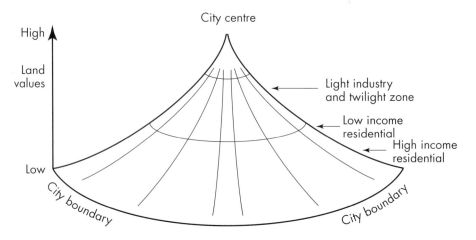

(i) What do the letters CBD stand for?

(ii) What does a *residential* area mean?

(iii) Where in the city are most shops found?

(iv) Why is this a good place to have shops?

(Edexcel)

14 Soils, vegetation and environments

Afforestation	Gley
Calcification	Gully
Canopy	Habitat
Chernozem	Hazard (environmental)
Climax vegetation	Horizon
Conservation	Humus
Deforestation	Landfill
Desertification	Leaching
Dynamism	Loess
Ecology	Natural resource
Ecosystem	Natural vegetation
Environmental quality monitoring	Podsol
Environmentally sensitive area	Pollution
(ESA)	Profile
Fertility	Rainforest
Fragile environment	Sahel

Saltmarsh
Savanna
Sere
Silt
Soil acidity
Soil conservation
Soil creep
Soil erosion
Soil profile
Soil texture

Succession
Taiga
Tree line
Tropical desert
Tropical grassland
Tundra
Wetland
Xerophyte
Zonal soil

GCSE example question: 14 Soils, vegetation and environments

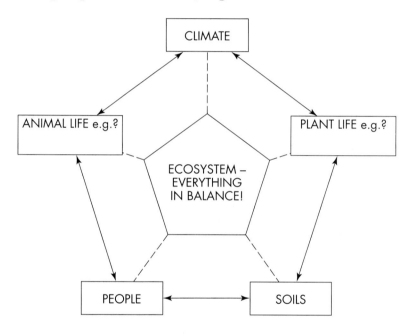

(a) The diagram above shows a model of an *ecosystem*. State the meaning of the term ecosystem.
(b) For a tropical rainforest, or another named ecosystem you have studied:
  (i) State *one named plant* and *one named animal* in this ecosystem;
  (ii) State fully *two* ways in which the activities of *people* could have a *destructive* effect upon the plants and animals in the ecosystem you have chosen.

(NISEC)

15 Transport and trade

Accessibility

Balance of trade

Break of bulk

Commuting

Distance-decay

Distribution

Export

Friction of distance

Globalisation

Import

Interdependence

Network/Transport network

Node

Park-and-ride

Pedestrianisation

Protectionism

Rapid transit system

Ro-ro

Route

Specialisation

Tariff

Trade

Trading bloc

Tramway

Visible trade

GCSE example question: 15 Transport and trade

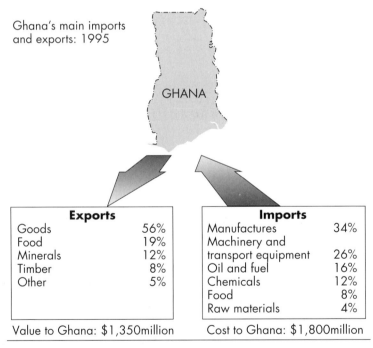

Ghana's main imports and exports: 1995

GHANA

Exports	
Goods	56%
Food	19%
Minerals	12%
Timber	8%
Other	5%

Imports	
Manufactures	34%
Machinery and transport equipment	26%
Oil and fuel	16%
Chemicals	12%
Food	8%
Raw materials	4%

Value to Ghana: $1,350million   Cost to Ghana: $1,800million

(a) (i) What is meant by the terms export and import?

    (ii) Name Ghana's main export and main import.

(b) Suggest a major difference between the kind of goods that are exported by Ghana and those that are imported.

(c) Ghana is a less economically developed country (LEDC). What economic problems does the trade pattern shown create for such a country?

ANSWERS TO GCSE QUESTIONS IN APPENDIX 1.

QUESTION 1

(a) (i) Commercial farming.
(ii) Any two of commercial farming; subsistence farming; shifting cultivation; nomadic herding. (iii) Any one of Africa; South America; Asia.
(b) (i) Subsistence farming.
(ii) Nomadic herding. (iii) Shifting cultivation. (iv) Commercal farming.
(c) (i) Low income: subsistence farming. Moderate income: peasant farming. High income: commercial farming.
(ii) Whichever pair you chose, you must say either why the level of income/development causes the farming type (e.g. low incomes mean that fertilisers and modern technology are not available so farm production remains low and little or none is left over for selling i.e. subsistence farming) or why farming type helps to cause level of income/development (e.g. countries can earn income from abroad by selling farm products there i.e. commercial farming helps to raise income levels).

QUESTION 2

(a) Depression. Cyclone and Low are also acceptable.
(b) (i) Arrow needs to point to the right.
(ii) Warm front; Cold front.
(c) B, E, C.
(d) Low.

QUESTION 3

(a)   A = cave; B = arch (natural); C = stack; D = wave-cut platform.

(b) You should have explained a sequence of events, starting with a cave (A) forming at a weak point in the cliff. The cave cuts backwards and gets eroded upwards to form an arch (B). Eventually, the arch collapses above leaving the seaward side standing alone as a stack (C). A sequence of diagrams should either form your entire answer or support a written answer. For example, your first diagram should show a headland with a cave forming, and so on.

(a) (i) Resources given to LEDCs to relieve emergencies e.g. famines. (ii) Clothing or portable lavatories. (iii) Money or resources given or lent on favourable terms and intended to promote economic development and improve quality of life e.g. by funding irrigation, education and transport schemes.

(b) (i) Tied aid. (ii) This type of deal improves British exports because financial aid may have to be spent on British goods; it may be in the form of loans earning interest. (iii) There are strings attached and therefore little freedom of choice.

QUESTION 5

(a) Power from any source that replenishes itself (i.e. never runs out).

(b) Wave or hydro-electric power.

(c) Electricity is cheaper to transport on a large scale than coal; electricity is more flexible to use than coal in homes (e.g. many appliances run on electricity); coal burning in all homes would result in atmospheric pollution.

QUESTION 6

(a) A = Pyramidal peak; B = corrie; C = hanging valley; D = ribbon lake.

(b) Long, narrow ribbon or finger lake in a U-shaped valley (glacial trough). This valley or trough dictates the shape of the lake.

QUESTION 7

(a) Chemical works = secondary; Historic ship centre = tertiary; Telephone call centre = tertiary; Oil refinery = secondary.

(b) (i) Bank clerk = formal; Shoe shine person = informal; Street car washer = informal; Government official = formal; Street food seller = informal.
(ii) Formal jobs = contract of employment; person pays taxes. Informal jobs = casual and irregular work; perhaps self-employed and person does not pay taxes.

(c) Accessible and suitable for a car-owning society. Conveniently close to major roads for one-stop shoppers in their cars, and large delivery lorries. Space for large car parks.

(d) Using these brownfield sites – old and derelict – can be: cheaper – nobody wants them; buildings may need only modernising; part of urban redevelopment and smartening up'; useful in taking pressure off, greenfield land. Why build on countryside on the edge of a town when there is building land in the town not now being used?

QUESTION 8

(a) Any named manufacturing industry is suitable e.g. chemicals, steel, cars.
    (i) Inputs = raw materials and/or components e.g. oil for chemicals; sheet
    steel for cars; (ii) Processes = factory processing and transport e.g. robots
    on car assembly line; furnaces and rolling mills, etc. for steel processing;
    (iii) Outputs = finished products that can be transported to market for
    sale e.g. plastics, acids, drugs from chemical industry.

(b) Local and national government encourage industries to certain locations,
    usually where there is unemployment and lower living standards. They
    place advertisements, offer financial support (e.g. grants for training;
    rent-free factories) talk persuasively to foreign companies, improve the
    infrastructure for companies, etc. (You should mention assisted or
    development areas.) Financial help is also available from the European
    Regional Development Fund in EU countries.

QUESTION 9

(a) (i) Primary = 60; Secondary = 28; Tertiary = 12. (ii) Jamaica is around A
    on the triangular graph.

(b) (i) Farming; fishing; quarrying. (ii) Factory worker of any type. (iii)
    Teaching; Medicine.

(c) First, the primary sector shrinks as the secondary sector grows. Later,
    the tertiary sector grows at the expense of the secondary sector. LEDCs
    tend to have large primary sectors and MEDCs large tertiary sectors. In
    MEDCs food, raw materials and goods are plentiful so services (tertiary
    sector) grow. In LEDCs there is still a demand for primary products and
    goods, so primary and secondary sectors remain large.

QUESTION 10

(i) D   (ii) B   (iii) C   (iv) E.

QUESTION 11

(a) (i) List A title – Natural; List B title – Human. (ii) List A – Climate;
    Relief; Water supplies. List B – Industry; Political decisions. (iii) The
    number of people living in an average square kilometre.

(b) (i) California coast and SE England are densely populated; Scottish
    Highlands and Sahara Desert are sparsely populated. (ii) Your answer
    should explain how some of the eight factors given in your completed
    Lists A and B cause the population density to be either high or low in
    your chosen area. For example, Scottish Highlands – rugged mountains
    with steep slopes unsuitable for building and lower temperatures
    unsuitable for some types of forming.

(a) (i) 5–6 hours. (ii) Most of rainfall does not fall directly into river; run-off from a catchment area takes time.

(b) (i) Near a river's source, vertical erosion produces a valley deep in relation to its width; near a river's mouth lateral erosion is stronger than vertical erosion and the valley is wide in relation to depth. Valleys widen downstream. (ii) Diagram of a wide, shallow river channel with labels showing: river overflowing its banks; silt deposited in flooded area where water flows much more slowly than in the river; silt left as a bank; bank grows as a result of successive flooding; levee forms river bank; river may now be above surrounding flood plain.

(c) Urban area means: infiltration less so run-off more because of concrete and tarmac; run-off rapid after rainfall so all the water enters the river at once; river channel may now be narrower or drainage may be straight into river.

(d) Less warning is given to people likely to be affected; more people live in simpler accommodation close to the river; less technology to cope with the effects of flooding. Flooding of Chinese rivers e.g. Yangtze is a good case study to use.

QUESTION 13

(i) Central business district. (ii) Housing. (iii) The CBD. Out-of-town retail complex would also be accepted e.g. The Meadowhall, Sheffield. (iv) Shops can expect large numbers of customers due to the accessibility of CBD by public transport and via the road network (an out-of-town retail complex offers high accessibility by car). The resulting high levels of turnover enable shops on a CBD or out-of-town complex to sustain the correspondingly high cost of buying or renting land there.

QUESTION 14

(a) A unit made up of living organisms and the non-living, or physical environment with which they interact.

(b) For a tropical rainforest: (i) Plant (e.g. liana, epiphyte); animal (e.g. monkey). (ii) Logging for hardwood for building purposes destroys trees that have taken centuries to grow, and will not be replaced; forest clearance for road building results in loss of many plant and animal habitats.

(a) (i) Export – goods or services produced in one country and sold to another; import – goods or services that one country purchases from another. (ii) Cocoa; Manufactures.
(b) Primary products are exported, and goods (processed products – secondary industry) are mostly imported.
(c) Imports are more valuable than exports so a trade deficit results; there is too much reliance on one primary product; as long as Ghana is importing processed products there is less incentive to develop its own manufacturing industry, which is, in general, a main source of economic development.

COMMAND WORDS USED IN QUESTIONS

One of the major pitfalls that face candidates in any examination is their difficulty in interpreting the demands of the questions asked of them. Thorough revision is essential, but candidates also require an awareness of what is expected from them in the examination itself. Too often candidates attempt to answer the question they think is there rather than the one which is actually set. Answering an examination question is challenging enough, without the extra self-imposed handicap of having misread the question.

Examiners always try to set questions which are clear in what they ask for, and can be answered by everyone who has followed the course and prepared adequately for the examination. It is not in the interest of the examiner for a question to be read ambiguously, or to be answered by only a few candidates.

Correct interpretation of the **Command words** of a question is therefore very important. In a GCSE geography examination paper, a variety of common words are used. Some command words demand more of the candidate than others. Some require a simple task to be performed, others require greater thought. There is, therefore, a hierarchy of command words. What follows is an attempt to describe what is required of the candidate by some of the major Command Words used in a geography examination.

Annotate means you should add labels or notes or short comments to an illustration.

Calculate means that a numerical answer is required. In general, your working should be shown.

Compare asks you to set out the factual details to show how far things either agree/disagree or are alike/unalike.

Complete requires you to add the remaining detail or details required to a written statement or an illustration.

Contrast asks you to identify differences.

Define or **state the meaning of** or **what is meant by** all require you to describe accurately, giving the meaning or definition of the concept in question.

Describe: this means you should set out the factual details of the subject. You should meet written specific requirement, to give account of something in terms of size, shape, height, etc. May also be seen as **Give an account of**.

Devise or **Plan** asks you to present a particular feature such as a form or questionnaire to meet a specific requirement or requirements.

Draw means you should make a sketch. Often coupled with a labelled diagram (draw a diagram/illustration with labels to identify its features).

Explain or **account for** asks you to give reasons for a particular feature.

Factor: characteristics bringing about certain result.

Feature: a characteristic of.

Giving your views: here you are being invited to say what you think about a subject.

How: In what way? To what extent? By what means/method? May be coupled with show how, prove how, demonstrate how.

Identify: here you are being asked to select, ascertain, recognise a specific feature or features on an illustration or in a written statement.

Illustrating your answer: you should give specific examples or diagrams in your answer.

Insert or **label** means you should place specific names or details on an illustration in response to a particular requirement.

List asks you to identify and name a number of features to meet a particular purpose.

Locate asks you to find the place of.

Mark means that you should indicate or show on an illustration a particular feature or features.

Match: here you should identify two or more statements or illustrations in which there is an element of similarity or inter-relationship (link).

Measure: this command implies that the quantity concerned can be directly obtained from a suitable measuring instrument.

Name: here you should state or specify or identify i.e. give the word or words by which a specific feature is known or give examples which illustrate a particular feature.

Pattern: a particular arrangement or distribution of items e.g. settlements. You may be asked to suggest a pattern or identify a pattern (or trend).

Reasons: you should explain, justify, give the causes of.

Refer to or **with reference to** means that you should write an answer which uses some of the ideas provided in an illustration, or other additional material such as a case study.

State asks you to set down in brief detail i.e. refer to an aspect of a particular feature by a short statement or by words or by a single word.

Study asks you to examine closely; pay special attention to; look carefully at and interpret.

Suggest: you should set down your ideas on or knowledge of; propose; put forward for consideration.

Use or **using the information provided:** base your answer on the information provided (on the content of an illustration or a written statement).

With the help of information in: write your answer using some of the information provided in the illustration as well as additional material.

These command or action words are just as important to your answer as the geographical words in the question, such as earthquake, migration or urbanisation. They tell you what aspect of earthquakes or migration or urbanisation the examiner expects you to write about; make sure, as you write, that you are doing so.

RESEARCHING AND WRITING A FIELDWORK ENQUIRY REPORT

What is important in geography cannot always be measured by written papers alone. Some skills are best assessed in a continuous way rather than in a few hours on the day of the examination. Coursework is mostly testing skills, as Table 1 for the SEG syllabus 'A' shows; 15 of the 25 marks from coursework are for skills, many of which cannot be tested in a written paper. Allowing marks for coursework is fairer to students who might suffer from exam nerves, and rewards work achieved during the course when there are not the same time limits on you. We all know that timed written exams have strong elements of a lottery. You may have a heavy cold or period, or the examiner may set the 'wrong' questions for you! By the time you get to the final written exam in GCSE, you will already have some marks under your belt from the coursework, so you will not be leaving your entire fate to the 'do-or-die' lottery of the exam.

Table 1 SEG Geography syllabus A

Objectives	Component			Total
	Written component one	Written component two	Coursework component	
Knowledge	12%	18%	–	30%
Understanding	11%	9%	10%	30%
Skills	17%	8%	15%	40%
Weighting of each component	40%	35%	25%	100%

All syllabuses have either 20 or 25% of the total marks for coursework. It is clearly a very important element in GCSE, and is generally a very effective means by which your abilities can be differentiated from those of your fellow students.

Coursework can be made suitable to your circumstances, abilities and interests, either by the teacher planning the work or by organising things so that you can choose your own topic and method of investigation.

Do complete the necessary amount of coursework! You cannot afford to lose marks by leaving work unfinished. The GCSE examining groups generally do not insist that all the coursework asked for in the syllabus be submitted before a grade can be awarded, but don't throw marks away! Make sure you submit for assessment the completed work.

Being judged on work done during the course does put strains and pressures on you, especially if you are the industrious type. Some students have an enormous amount of work which is very demanding on their time. You will need to be very organised and to allocate plenty of time to coursework. Don't panic and don't let it get you down!

You will need to earn to work independently, and to organise your time. Remember coursework will be completed in your own time. Know exactly when coursework must be given in! Then produce a 'deadline diary' for yourself, entering the dates when each piece should be handed in. Include all your coursework in all your subjects. Parents can help with this diary or you can ask your teacher. Next, plan exactly when you are going to do each piece of work and set yourself check dates by which time you should have reached a certain point in your investigation. If you can keep up to date, then you might avoid conflict over the use of your time for other pieces of coursework, revision and your social life. To keep up to date, you will need to be able to motivate yourself to get down to work and keep at it, pacing yourself correctly. Good working habits and support from your parents (e.g. by providing funds and transport if you have to go out and collect the data for your fieldwork enquiry) are enormous help. Try to arrange a shelf and/or a series of files at home where you can keep your coursework as it accumulates.

Coursework is marked by your own teacher, according to strict guidelines produced by the examining group. Table 2 is an outline example from the NEAB. The marks are then moderated by an examiner who reassesses some or all of the work from your school or college. This ensures that the marks conform to standards elsewhere. The examiner will change your teacher's marks, if necessary, so that everyone's work is marked according to the same standards.

Table 2 A mark scheme for the geographical fieldwork investigation (NEAB Syllabus A)

	Mark
A Planning and organisation: how well the candidates handled the investigation as a whole, including problem identification and the generation of hypotheses.	9
B Observation, collection and recording of data, and sorting of secondary data.	12
C Classification and representation of the information using relevant techniques and presentation, and description of secondary data.	12
D The skills involving interpretation of the transformed data and the ability to analyse and make judgements leading to valid conclusions.	24
E Spelling, punctuation and grammar.	3
Total mark.	60

The number of pieces of coursework you must do does vary from syllabus to syllabus. Four of the twelve syllabuses (London 'A, NEAB 'A' and 'B' and NICCEA) ask for one piece; three (London 'B', MEG 'B' and 'C') ask for two pieces; and the other five offer a choice of one or two pieces. Whether it is to be one or two pieces, your coursework must include a geographical investigation supported by at least two days' fieldwork, spent collecting 'first hand' data in a small area, usually in your local environment.

Geographical enquiry is a part of everyone's GCSE geography course. The enquiry skills involved in planning and carrying out a fieldwork investigation are tested in all the syllabuses. Every syllabus asks you to complete at least one geographical investigation, which may either be teacher-directed and already planned in outline, or more of your own choosing. There are six stages through which you must go to complete an enquiry. This is often known as the enquiry sequence or the scientific method, because it is the way in which scientists think and work. Sometimes it is called the research design, because it is the way in which researchers carry out their work. Coursework in GCSE geography is largely about you going through each of these processes, and the teacher and examiner assessing your performance in each enquiry skill.

The enquiry approach is a means by which a question, problem, hypothesis, situation, conflict or issue can be investigated methodically in a series of steps, starting with a defined aim and progressing to a conclusion, taking into consideration the information gathered during the investigation.

Table 3 shows the stages through which your investigation should go.

Table 3 The enquiry sequence

Stage 1	Identifying a problem or hypothesis or issue or question
Stage 2	Selecting appropriaie methods
Stage 3	Collecting relevant data
Stage 4	Analysing the data
Stage 5	Interpreting the data
Stage 6	Reporting findings and conclusions

Writing up your completed investigation should include the following seven sections.

1 **Title:** e.g. 'Does our town need a bypass?' 'Rivers flow faster the further they are from their source'.
2 **Aims:** explain in your own words what you are trying to discover.

3 **Methods:** describe how you collect the data, both field and secondary (see below); explain why you collected it; comment on its suitability.

4 **Presentation of data:** use a variety of techniques (e.g. tables, bar charts, averages, etc.) to illustrate your data or a selection drawn from it.

5 **Analysis and interpretation:** what does the 'presentation section' suggest; are there any trends, deviations from trend, etc.?

6 **Conclusion:** summarise your findings, relating back to your aims.

7 **Appendix:** include your rough fieldwork notes and a bibliography.

An investigation should be planned in this order and written up in this order, using these headings. It will be marked this way, as Table 2 above shows. The vast bulk of geography coursework calls for enquiry work. Your teacher will tell you if any coursework does not require the enquiry approach. No investigation should be left entirely to you. You will need your teacher's guidance in selecting the investigation (when it is not a teacher-directed one) and in deciding what approach, surveys and data collection are necessary.

Generally speaking, a good piece of geography coursework will have the following:

1 IT ADOPTS THE 'RIGHT' APPROACH

Geography coursework should involve student enquiry. 'Look-see-describe' fieldwork reports, full of copied material and 'stick-ins', are out! We have shown what is meant by an enquiry approach. Your written-up study should be arranged in the seven sections shown above, which incorporates the elements considered in Table 2.

Start with an explanation of what you set out to try to do; then describe your methods; then present the data you collected in diagrams, maps, etc. (it is a good idea to put your original data in an appendix at the back of the study); include an analysis of your results where you interpret and discuss your data; finish with a conclusion which is linked to your original purpose behind the work. Writing the work up in this way will show the examiner that you have adopted an enquiry-based approach. Try to have a clear, snappy title, perhaps best written right at the end when the work is done, and in the form of either a question, a hypothesis (i.e. a geographical statement) which testing will either prove or disprove, or a problem/issue. Examples might be: 'inner city areas are deprived areas', or 'the growth of retail parks/out-of-town shopping centres reflects our changing life styles'.

Route to fieldwork investigation
(NEAB syllabus C)

Stage of production	Student activity
Identification of the issues or questions. Preparation	Students or class discuss the feasibility and planning with their teacher. Students write up their introduction.
Primary data collection, observation, recording, sketching, mapping, etc. Selection and collation of data/information	Students or class carry out fieldwork, collate and select data/information. Students provide evidence of their own fieldwork activity. Individuals write up and evaluate method
Representation and communication of results	Students may seek teacher guidance. Students represent and communicate their results.
Analysis and interpretation of results.	Students analyse, interpret and draw conclusions about their findings.
Completion and review.	Students organise and complete the work and review their findings.

2 IT IS ACTUALLY BASED ON FIELDWORK

This is vital where the syllabus calls for fieldwork enquiry. You should check with your teacher whether fieldwork is required or not. Fieldwork means that you observe, collect and record your data yourself, outside the classroom; this data will be first-hand information, known as primary data. Filling in questionnaires in the street, or taking measurements on the bank of the river, produces primary data. Secondary data is that collected by other people so that it comes to you second-hand. Information that you might take from a population census, or from Meteorological Office weather records, can be used to support your primary data in a fieldwork enquiry, but for a fieldwork enquiry there must be primary data with it! Some coursework for GCSE can be based on secondary data alone, but this will not then be a fieldwork investigation.

Such secondary source enquiries based on sources like directories, published maps, official statistics etc. and conducted entirely in classrooms or at home make suitable second pieces of coursework where the syllabus calls for two pieces.

3 IT INCLUDES THE VARIOUS TYPES OF GEOGRAPHY WHICH THE EXAMINATION BOARD SAYS IT WILL GIVE MARKS FOR

It will be impossible for you to gain the marks set aside for values or skills when these are missing from your coursework. Your overall coursework should include a lot of practical skills work, including as many suitable techniques of presentation as possible, and some work which shows your understanding and awareness of peoples' values. Investigations which consider a conflict of interest between two groups of people like residents and a business community might fit the bill.

4 IT IS VERY LARGELY YOUR OWN WORK

It is important that both you and your teacher can sign a declaration that your investigation is largely your own work. This should not stop you from regularly consulting your teacher about how a fieldwork investigation is coming along, about what you might do next, etc. Your teachers cannot do the work for you but they are there to help and guide you! Equally, it is quite acceptable for data to be collected in groups and for you then to pool and share it, provided that the rest of the work – the presentation of the data, its analysis and the conclusions drawn from it – is your own personal work.

5 IT IS OF A SUITABLE LENGTH

It is quality rather than quantity that counts in GCSE! Syllabuses recommend that coursework should be kept down to between 2000 and 3000 words, including your maps and diagrams. This is no more than between eight and 15 sides of A4 paper. You must not forget that, although coursework studies should not be long in terms of pages of written work, they should be long in terms of the time you spend on the work. Coursework does carry a large percentage of the final marks for the examination: at least 20%.

Finally, a word about the actual submission of your coursework. Try to make everything you submit as impressive to look at as possible. The presentation of your work is very important. Research has shown that examiners give the same work higher marks when it is written neatly and is legible, than when it is in a mess. Here are a few tips to help you to present your coursework decently:

1 Make sure that each section is completed, and has a clear and proper heading.
2 Check that all maps and diagrams are correctly labelled and have a title, a key, a scale, etc.
3 Read the whole of your coursework through at least once, watching out for careless errors. Check that the introduction and conclusion describe the study accurately, that you have stated your findings clearly and that the points you make follow on from one another sensibly. Make sure that your work demonstrates what it is supposed to. Rewrite any parts that you are unhappy with.

The following *GCSE A–Z Handbooks* are available from Hodder & Stoughton. Why not use them to support your other GCSE and Intermediate GNVQs? All the *A–Zs* are written by experienced authors and Chief Examiners.

0 340 73060 9 *GCSE A–Z Double Science* £7.99
0 340 68366 X *GCSE A–Z Business Studies* £7.99
0 340 753579 *GCSE A–Z Biology* £7.99 (September 1999)

All Hodder & Stoughton *Educational* books are available at your local bookshop, or can be ordered direct from the publisher. Just tick the titles you would like and complete the details below. Prices and availability are subject to change without prior notice.

Buy four books from the selection above and get free postage and packing. Just send a cheque or postal order made payable to *Bookpoint Limited* to the value of the total cover price of the books including postage and packaging. This should be sent to: Hodder & Stoughton *Educational*, 39 Milton Park, Abingdon, Oxon OX14 4TD, UK. EMail address: orders@bookpoint.co.uk. The following postage and packaging costs apply:

UK & BFPO: £4.30 for one book; £6.30 for two books; £8.30 for three books.
Overseas and Eire: £4.80 for one book; £7.10 for 2 or 3 books (surface mail).

If you would like to pay by credit card, our centre team would be delighted to take your order by telephone. Our direct line (44) 01235 827720 (lines open 9.00am - 6.00pm, Monday to Saturday, with a 24 hour answering service). Alternatively you can send a fax to (44) 01235 400454.

Title _____ First name _____ Surname _____

Address _____

Postcode _____ Daytime telephone no. _____

If you would prefer to pay by credit card, please complete:

Please debit my Master Card / Access / Diner's Card / American Express (delete as applicable)

Card number _____ Expiry date _____ Signature _____

If you would not like to receive further information on our products, please tick the box
☐